Tend And Feed, Tend And Feed

Cycle C Sermons Based on the Gospel Lessons for Advent, Christmas, and Epiphany

John B. Jamison

CSS Publishing Company, Inc.
Lima, Ohio

TEND AND FEED, TEND AND FEED

FIRST EDITION
Copyright © 2021
by CSS Publishing Co., Inc.

Library of Congress Cataloging-in-Publication Data:

Names: Jamison, John B., 1952- author. Title: Tend and feed, tend and feed : Cycle C sermons based gospel lessons for Advent, Christmas, and Epiphany / John B. Jamison. Other titles: Sermons. Selections. Description: First edition. | Lima, Ohio : CSS Publishing Company, Inc., [2021] Identifiers: LCCN 2020055171 | ISBN 9780788030185 (paperback) | ISBN 9780788030192 (ebook) Subjects: LCSH: Bible. Gospels--Sermons. | Common lectionary (1992). Year C. | Church year sermons. | Advent sermons. | Christmas sermons. | Epiphany--Sermons. Classification: LCC BS2555.54 .J36 2021 | DDC 252/.61--dc23 LC record available at https://lccn.loc.gov/2020055171

For more information about CSS Publishing Company resources, visit our website at www. csspub.com, email us at csr@csspub.com, or call (800) 241-4056.

e-book:
ISBN-13: 978-0-7880-3019-2
ISBN-10: 0-7880-3019-1

ISBN-13: 978-0-7880-3018-5
ISBN-10: 0-7880-3018-3   DIGITALLY PRINTED

For Pat, whose tending and feeding helps me retell the stories.

Contents

Maybe Today   9
First Sunday of Advent
Luke 21:25-36

You Sent Who?   15
Second Sunday of Advent
Luke 3:1-6

Fruit Production   21
Third Sunday of Advent
Luke 3:7-18

Redefining Blessed   26
Fourth Sunday of Advent
Luke 1:39-46 (46-55)

POW!   32
Nativity of the Lord
Luke 2(1-7); 8-20

Finding The Sermon   38
First Sunday after Christmas Day
Luke 2:41-52

Seating Arrangements   44
New Year's Day
Matthew 25:31-46

Words   49
Second Sunday after Christmas
John 1(1-9); 10-18

That Moment In Time   55
Epiphany of the Lord
Matthew 2:1-12

Learning Our Role 60
Baptism of the Lord / First Sunday after the Epiphany
Luke 3:15-17, 21-22

Who Is This Jesus? 67
Second Sunday after the Epiphany
John2:1-11

Going Home – Part One: Which Me Will It Be? 74
Third Sunday after the Epiphany
Luke 4:14-21

Going Home – Part Two: Then And Now 78
Fourth Sunday after the Epiphany
Luke 4:21-30

Doing What Matters 83
Fifth Sunday after the Epiphany
Luke 5:1-11

Two Lives To Live 88
Sixth Sunday after the Epiphany
Luke 6:17-26

The List 95
Seventh Sunday after the Epiphany
Luke 6:27-38

When Following Is Not Enough 101
Transfiguration Sunday
Luke 9:28-36, (37-43a)

God's Algorithm 106
Eighth Sunday after the Epiphany
Luke 6:39-49

A Slap In The Face 111
Ninth Sunday after the Epiphany
Luke 7:1-10

Preface

Over the weeks that I prepared these messages, the news was filled to overflowing with stories of anger, suspicion, division, and expressions that were as near pure hatred as I have witnessed. As I turned from the news to re-read these passages of scripture, while I was certainly trying to come up with sermon topics, my personal goal was to see if I could hear some word of hope, some word of the direction Jesus would offer if he was the subject of one of those constant media interviews. I read about prophecy, miracles, confrontations, blessings, woes, and all the rest; all-important, yet not offering me the simple and clear message my mind imagined Jesus would offer. He had such a gift for cutting through the noise, calling a snake a snake, and saying the very words that needed to be heard, so that was what I was hoping to hear.

Finally, I heard it. I realize it may just be the words that I needed to hear, and if you hear something else in these passages, I encourage you to modify these messages to make them your own. But what I heard speaking to me over and over through these passages is that above and beyond anything else we might talk about, the one thing that defines whether I am living my life as a disciple of Jesus Christ is very simple: am I tending to, and am I feeding God's sheep? Not in some philosophical way, that we might redefine what it means to "tend" and to "feed." Just tend, and just feed. That's it. And what sheep? All sheep. Whoever, wherever, whatever they may believe, whatever policy or issue they may or may not support. My life is being defined by who I am willing to tend and feed. That is what I hear Jesus saying to me in each of these passages, so that is what I offer to you.

Tend and feed.
Tend and feed.

Maybe Today…

"Maybe today."

He stood at the window and watched the morning sun climb over the mountain. He lowered his eyes to shield them from the glare of the sunlight shining against the streets and buildings. It was a bright and beautiful morning, but all he felt was darkness. It was the same darkness he had felt last night as he tried to sleep. It was the same darkness he felt every day now, the same one that they all felt every day now.

He raised his eyes to the window again.

"Maybe today," he said.

He stepped from his house to go to work. Along his way, he was very careful to be aware of his surroundings. Every day, he heard the stories of what had happened to others; some from his own neighborhood. The fortunate ones had been stopped by one of the official security groups who had forced them to show some proof of who they were and where they were going. Some of them had been ordered to carry things for the groups, give them their coat, shoes, or in some other way demonstrate their loyalty to the country and its leaders. But there were laws that controlled the actions of the official security groups, so while the experience was frightening and frustrating, it was something that could be endured until God finally put an end to it.

The less fortunate ones had been stopped by one of the unofficial groups who were patrolling the city. These groups did not have or care about laws that might control their behavior. Some of the neighbors who had been stopped by these groups were put into wagons and carried away. Some were questioned and beaten, and then let go to warn others of what they faced.

Some were carried away to simply disappear.

Even in the brightness of the morning sunlight, the streets were a place of darkness.

And sometimes, the darkness came inside. As he walked, he remembered the stories he had heard about how the security groups had sometimes forced their way into people's homes. Maybe someone had accused them of disloyalty, or perhaps they had been overheard saying something that was considered disloyal. And that led to doorways being broken-down in the middle of the night, and someone being carried away for investigation, or worse.

"Maybe today," he said.

He turned the corner and saw the sunlight shining on the great, golden columns of the temple. It was a sight that used to give him a feeling of pride and great hope. But now, the people controlling the temple were working with those who sent the security groups into the streets. As he turned away from the view of the temple and entered his office, all he felt was disappointment.

"Maybe today," he said.

For many, life in the first century was living in darkness. Things that had once given comfort and hope, like the Jerusalem temple, now just hurt to look at and think about. The community of neighbors that had meant so much to them was now a place of division and suspicion. Even their faith community was broken, divided by frustration and anger, and the temple was a place where those who openly spoke of God acting to overcome oppression did that at the risk of being reported to one of the security groups.

Even family, the core of everything that had meaning for them, was being ripped apart.

The people in first-century Jerusalem awoke each day knowing they were under the control of a people who did not like them, who did not trust them, who did not believe those under their control had the right to be who they believed they were. They were under the control of people who believed that their own beliefs and lives were the only ones of value, and those under their control must be forced to obey, whatever it took.

The Roman empire was an efficient ruler. When a new land was conquered, a local governor was assigned to maintain order and bring that land into compliance with the rest of the empire. If the governor wanted to keep his job, the one thing he had to do was make sure there was never any act of resistance that would be reported back to Rome. So the primary goal was to do whatever needed to be done to keep the people from resisting. Whatever was needed. The governor had his forces, well-trained centurions who knew how to follow orders and do what needed to be done to intimidate and subdue any resistance.

If the conquered land had a government or key religion, Rome did not demand that those things be stopped; just that they offered no resistance to the Roman leadership. In fact, Rome was more than willing to partner with existing political and religious leaders, offering grand incentives to those leaders who were willing to do so. That is why the temple still shone in the morning sunlight. The leaders of the temple were allowed to continue their religious activities on two key conditions. First, they did nothing that might disrupt the peaceful obedience to Roman rule. And second, the temple leaders paid the empire a percentage of whatever money they brought in.

The other community and religious leaders were offered the same conditions. Groups like the Pharisees and Sadducees would be allowed to maintain their roles as leaders and pillars of the community, and to keep their wealth, so long as they did not encourage any disruption against the government themselves or stop anyone who tried. Those who had once been responsible for interpreting and teaching the faith to serve God had now become responsible for interpreting and teaching that faith to serve the government.

Rome was also very good at finding and using the unofficial and usually radical groups that existed behind the scenes in every land. These groups were offered the recognition they all sought, in return for doing whatever they might do to instill fear in the people and put a quick end to any resistance against Rome that might arise.

Rome had its direct methods of reminding the community of their powerlessness against the empire. A Roman centurion could stop any citizen on the street and force them to carry their things for them, or force them to give them their coat, their shoes, or anything else.

However harsh Rome may have been, there were still laws that limited just how far a centurion could go in their intimidation. That was not the case for the unofficial security groups. They could do whatever they wanted to do, so long as they did those things in ways that did not lead to a meaningful resistance from anyone.

In the past, when the nation was threatened, the people looked to the temple and the priests for God's guidance. They looked to their leaders and teachers to hear what the scriptures directed them to do. Today, all they could find to give them the hope they sought were the old words of prophets like Isaiah, Jeremiah, and Joel — words saying that one day, God would fulfill the promises made and come with the mighty armies of heaven and destroy those who oppress God's people. One day, the sky will break open, the oppressors will be swept from the temple, from the streets, from the entire land, and the people will once again be free to be God's own people as they were meant to be.

One day.

Maybe today.

Maybe today, God will act. Maybe today, we will see the Son of Man come on that cloud with power and glory and drive these enemies out of our land. Maybe today, God will send the heavenly armies and put an end to this darkness.

Maybe today.

Maybe today, after Jesus stood in the temple, right in front of everyone, and said that this very generation will not pass away until these things have happened. After all of this waiting, maybe it would be today.

So, we wait.

Advent is a season of waiting for God to act. The day will

come, God will act. Evil always loses in the end. So, we wait. The important question is, how do we wait? Some say march. Some say fight. Some say pray. What are we supposed to do while we wait for God to act?

Jesus said that what we need to do is be careful. But be careful of what? Jesus said we need to be careful that, when the evil is finally destroyed, we may still be able to stand before God. Be careful that, whatever we might do, we do not become a partner with the evil.

The danger of waiting for God to send some heavenly armies is that we buy into the idea of seeking vengeance. The great "so there!" It would be natural for us to feel that... perfectly justifiable to feel that... if we were not God's children. Vengeance is not ours to take, no matter how loudly it screams for us to claim it.

The greatest threat of evil, the greatest threat of the darkness we sometimes live in, is not that something might happen to us. The greatest threat we face is that we throw away the light we believe in and become just another creature of the dark.

We are not called to sit back, accept evil, and do nothing. We are called to do something far more difficult. We are called to remember who we are. We are called to remember who we are supposed to be — to remember to not allow anyone or anything to pull us into doing things only the evil ones would do. We are called to hold onto our love for our neighbor, even when it would be so easy to hate that neighbor. We are called to love our neighbor, even when that neighbor forgets about God, and sees us as anything other than a neighbor. We are told to tend and feed God's sheep.

There is simply no room in the human heart for both good and evil. The two cannot co-exist. We either love as God asks us to love, or we do not love. One is a heart of light, the other is a heart of darkness. Our greatest risk is to allow hatred a place in our heart.

Maybe today.

But if not today, we know with absolute certainty that this evil will come to a crashing and absolute end. Our greatest challenge as God's people is to see that we do not forget who we are, that we may avoid becoming the very thing that has created this darkness in the first place.

It may be the hardest thing we will ever do. But we know that one day, God will bring about change. And when that day comes, we will again look out the window at the morning light and feel the brightness inside. Amen.

Luke 3:1-6

You Sent Who?

Tiberius Caesar.
Pontius Pilate.
Herod Antipas.
Phillip the Tetrarch.
Annas.
Caiaphas.

These are the names of the first century; names that define a time and place. They are examples of the power of names and what they represent.

Tiberius Caesar had been emperor for fifteen years. Tiberius Caesar was the second Roman emperor after his stepfather Augustus Caesar. Tiberius Caesar was known as one of Rome's greatest generals, conquering the north as far as Germania, securing what would become the Roman northern frontier. He was not all that happy to be the emperor, but he knew how to use power very well.

Pontius Pilate was the fifteenth governor of Judea and was one of the longest-serving governors. That means he must have known how to keep Rome happy. The role of governor was officially a military position, but the forces he had were used more as a police force than an army. Pilate was the head of the judicial system and held the power to inflict capital punishment when he wanted to use it. He was responsible for collecting taxes, disbursing funds, and minting money. While he allowed the local religious court, the Sanhedrin, to continue in their role, he made sure that they kept him in the loop and did their part to keep the Jewish people under control and not let them stir up any trouble for him. Pilate's role of governor was officially under the rule of the Legate of Syria, but since there was no Legate of Syria for most of his time in office, he was free to do whatever he wanted to do.

Pilate's role was to keep the peace. To keep the Jewish people under control, whatever the cost. To demonstrate his control, in the dark of night, Pilate had banners brought into the city, displaying the symbols of the Roman empire simply to show his authority over the Jews. He took money from the temple treasury to pay for a water aqueduct for the city, and when the people protested, Pilate's police force came on horseback, carrying clubs. Many people died before the mobs were quieted.

Herod Antipas, the Tetrarch of Galilee, ruled over all of the land west of the Sea of Galilee. He was the son of Herod the Great, but he had not been the first choice as Tetrarch. While he was known as a skilled builder of cities, his behavior as a leader was questionable. He is perhaps remembered most for divorcing his wife so he could steal the wife of his half-brother. Not only was it questionable morally, since his wife was the daughter of a neighboring king, his actions ended up leading to a disastrous war with several nearby countries. He was eventually accused of conspiracy against the empire and exiled to Spain.

His brother Phillip was Tetrarch of the land east of the Sea of Galilee. He was loyal to the Roman empire, and since there were very few Jews in the land, his control was rarely challenged. As a result, his reign was for the most part a peaceful one.

Annas had been the high priest of the temple until Pilate replaced him after a disagreement. Pilate appointed Caiaphas as high priest. It is worth remembering that Caiaphas was Anna's son, one of five sons of Anna's who would serve as high priest. And since a high priest ruled for life, although Caiaphas was officially the high priest, Annas continue to have significant influence. Caiaphas followed his father's footsteps and had close connections with the Sanhedrin and with the Sadducees, the wealthy elite members of the land. Caiaphas served as high priest for eighteen years, which means he had a good working relationship with the Romans as well. That means he did what they wanted him to do.

Tiberius Caesar.

Pontius Pilate.

Herod Antipas.

Phillip the Tetrarch.

Annas.

Caiaphas.

These are the names of power in the first century. And the people wondered, "How do we stand against names like these? How do we respond to the power and abuse that these names represent? How will God overcome them?"

Those were the questions being asked by God's people in the first century. They believed that God would help them. But how? Who would God send?

They remembered God's great armies from scripture: the battles, the miracles, the fires, the brimstone, the floods, the locusts, the frogs. They knew that one of these days, God will act. They believed that one of these days, God would raise up a man who will show once and for all what real power is all about, because after all, that those who held power must be overthrown with power.

They talked about Moses, who was raised in Pharaoh's own house and used his position of power to free his people from oppression. They talked about David and Solomon, and how they used their power as kings to destroy enemies that threatened God's people. They talked about the words of Isaiah and Jeremiah and all of the others who wrote about God's heavenly armies of armed chariots of fire that would one day drive the enemy out of the land.

A voice of one calling in the wilderness,
'Prepare the way for the Lord,
make straight paths for him.
Every valley shall be filled in,
every mountain and hill made low.
The crooked roads shall become straight,

the rough ways smooth.
And all people will see God's salvation.

Isaiah 40:3-5 (NIV)

Now, that is power!

And they wondered who God would send this time. "Who will God send to free us? Who will God send to lead us in the great battle against those names of power that control us today? What role of power will that man come from? What God-given powers will that men bring with him?"

Herod, Pilate, Annas, Caiaphas, all knew what the people were thinking, and although they did not have the same belief that the Jewish god was going to act against them, they were determined to not allow anyone to challenge their control. The Roman empire knew how to deal with powerful threats. They had the armies, and they had the laws, and anyone who tried to act or speak against them with power was quickly silenced.

I have told you all of these things so I could read this one passage:

In the fifteenth year of the reign of Tiberius Caesar — when Pontius Pilate was governor of Judea, Herod Tetrarch of Galilee, his brother Philip Tetrarch of Iturea and Traconitis, and Lysanias Tetrarch of Abilene — during the high-priesthood of Annas and Caiaphas, the word of God came to John son of Zechariah in the wilderness.

Luke 3:1-3 (NRSV)

I gave that background so you would understand why, when God sent John the Baptist to the Jordan River, both the people of power and the people being oppressed said, "You sent who?"

The people making the trip to see John at the Jordan River expected to see power. Maybe it would be a leader of heavenly armies, or maybe it would be another Moses, using his family's position of power to do God's will. They expected to see the kind of power they all believed God would send to once and for all overcome those names that held the control.

Instead, they found a skinny man yelling at them from the middle of the river. Instead of heavenly armor, he wore a burlap bag with a piece of rope for a belt. Instead of a helmet of gold, his uncovered, water-soaked hair hung down his face, almost covering his wild-looking eyes. Instead of leading armies of angel-driven war chariots, he stood alone. He looked like someone who wandered the wilderness, surviving on bugs, berries, and whatever else he could scrounge-up. And that is exactly who he was.

And they all said, "You sent who?"

The members of the Sanhedrin, and the Pharisees, and other people of power who went to the Jordan River expected to see someone who might look powerful enough to be a threat. Someone with a family background with the wealth and connections to cause trouble. Someone with the appearance that would stir people into forming behind him to attack those in control.

Instead, they saw the same thing the people saw, and they all said to the imaginary Jewish God, "You sent who?"

It was one of God's great surprises.

Every generation has their list of names that represent the power that tries to control them, that tries to keep them from becoming who God asks them to be. I am sure we could list the names of our day as well.

And each generation is challenged to decide how God wants them to act against those in control, and what they are to do while they wait for God to come. How do we wait for God to act against an oppressor?

Do we try to overcome the names of power by using the same kinds of power they use? Do we look for leaders who have the same powers? Or do we do something different? Something surprising?

I suggest we remember two things:

First, everyone looked at John the Baptizer and shook their heads in disbelief, until he spoke.

And today, more than two-thousand years after that day, we might remember the names of Tiberius Caesar, Pontius Pilate, Herod Antipas, Phillip the Tetrarch, Annas, and Caiaphas, but it is John's name that represents the only true power that has survived.

So, it is Advent, and we wait.

We wait, knowing that one day soon, we are going to look at what God has done, and we are all going to say, "You sent who?"

Everyone will laugh.

And then that person will speak.

It is Advent, and we wait for God's big surprise!

Luke 3:7-18

Fruit Production

I'd like to tell you about a trip I made the other day, down to the Jordan. You know it isn't all that far, but it is a challenging walk, so I took plenty to drink and an extra jacket because I knew it would be cold by the time I get back. I threw a couple of snacks in my jacket pocket too, just in case I got hungry.

Well, I heard there were a lot of people planning on going, so I left Bethany early to avoid the crowd on the road. You know, some of those places along the road near Jericho are pretty narrow. I guess I should have left earlier because the roads were already crammed full of people when I got started.

Most everyone was walking, like me, but every once in a while someone would come along on a mule or with a wagon. Most of them moved slowly and carefully to give us walkers the chance to get out of the way, so it wasn't all that bad. But then a group of Pharisees, Sadducees, and priests from the temple came along. Of course, they were all decked out in their robes and tassels and were either riding on something or being carried by some of their servants. I'll tell you, they didn't slow down for anyone. They just yelled at people to get out of their way and moved on. I stopped several times to help someone who had been pushed off the side of the road. I think a lot of us thought about picking up a rock and heaving it at that group, but we all knew what would happen if we did.

Some people seemed surprised that the Pharisees, Sadducees, and priests would be going down to the Jordan like that, but I wasn't surprised at all. You know how those people are. Any time there is something going on where they can be seen in their fancy robes and stuff, they are going to go. And I said to someone that I bet when that group got down there, they would all be standing right out in front where everyone would see them.

But I also knew they would be there because any time they think someone might be trying to stir things up against them, they are going to show up to see if it looks like a real threat.

I finally got to the river around lunchtime and wow, the place was packed. There were people standing on both sides of the river, trying to get a good look at this John guy we had all heard about.

I saw people I knew from Bethany and Jerusalem, several from Bethlehem and Jericho, but there were a lot of others too. I heard there were people from as far north as Galilee, and there were even some Samaritans there. It was quite a crowd. But I'll tell you, there were no problems, even with the Samaritans there. Everyone was paying attention to John.

And, just like I expected, standing right in front by the edge of the river was that group of Pharisees, Sadducees, and priests. It was a lot warmer down there, so I took my jacket off and tucked it under my arm, but those guys still wore their heavy robes and hats to make sure everyone knew who they were.

I was trying to get close enough to hear and pay attention to what John was saying, but I was just really annoyed by those robes. Most of us were there to see if John could help us, but those guys up front were there just to protect themselves. We were all hoping and praying that, somehow, God might use John to bring peace. Those in the robes just wanted to find out if John was someone they needed to get rid of like they had gotten rid of the others.

Again, I thought for a second about moving down there and "accidentally" bumping one of those guys into the water, but I didn't. But I sure wanted to!

When I finally got close enough to get a good look at John, I wasn't sure what to think. I don't know what I was expecting, but it wasn't what I saw.

He stood out in the water and people were going up to him and being baptized, so they must have known more about him than I did so far. Some of them had heard him speak before, and some of them were even following him around as he traveled, so they must have believed he was something special, but I sure couldn't see it yet.

Some of the other people in the crowd must have felt the same way I did, because I heard a lot of them talking about it. The Pharisees, Sadducees, and priests must have felt the same because I saw them shaking their heads and turning to start the trip back to Jerusalem.

That's when John stopped baptizing people. He walked over to the edge of the river and looked at the crowd. Actually, he looked right at those robes.

Then he started talking.

And I have to tell you - that's when I knew.

Apparently, that's when the guys in robes knew too because when John was finished talking, they went back to Jerusalem and started figuring out how they were going to make him stop talking.

What did he say that scared them? I'll tell you. And to be honest with you, if we really think about what he said, we might almost feel the same way the Pharisees, Sadducees, and priests felt. Let me explain what I mean.

It was great at first. He started out by actually calling those robed people a bunch of snakes. I'll tell you, that made them stop and turn back around. You should have seen the looks on their faces.

You know that most of those guys in the robes got where they were because of their families, right? First Annas was high priest, now his son Caiaphas is high priest; they all got where they were because they can say their family tree goes way back, maybe all the way to Moses or even Abraham.

Well, John walked closer to them and said that their family background didn't mean a blasted thing to God. He said that he could pick up one of the stones in the river and turn it into a child of Abraham.

Then he really went at them. He told them that God wanted

us to produce good fruit and that God had an axe in his hand and was going to cut them down and throw them in a fire just like an old, dead, fruitless, tree.

That's when the whole bunch of them turned around and swished their fancy robes back up the road to Jerusalem. It was just so great to see those guys finally get what they deserved.

Did I tell you there were even some tax collectors there? I think it was one of them that finally asked John what he meant when he said that God wanted us to produce fruit? What kind of fruit? He asked John what we should do.

Well, you know how tax collectors are, don't you? They figure out how much tax we are supposed to pay, and then they add on a good percentage that they get to keep. John looked at the guy and told him to not collect any more taxes than he is required to collect. In other words, not to take anything for himself.

John looked around and said that we should not extort people and that we should not falsely accuse people of things. God wanted us to treat people fairly and honestly, which sounded really good.

But remember, I said that if we understood what John said, we might feel the same way the guys in robes felt. Well, that's because of the other things he said. It was great to hear him say what he did about the robes and tax collectors, but then he kept going. He looked around at all of us and said that anyone who has two shirts, should give one of those shirts to someone who doesn't have any shirt. There I was with my undershirt on, another shirt on top of it, and a jacket wrapped around my waist. Then he said that anyone who had food should do the same and give half of it to someone who didn't have any food. I kind of turned sideways a bit to hide the bulge from those snacks I put in my jacket pocket.

I just looked at him standing there. Did he really mean that he expected us all to do those things? To give away our clothes and our food? Yes, that is exactly what he meant.

When I went down there, I thought that God was going to send someone to drive out the Romans and the guys in robes, so we could get back to living the way we used to. But I was beginning to realize that what God was going to do was create a completely different way of living. We weren't going to think about where we are from, or what we have, or the things we might want to have. But we are supposed to think about what the others around us have, and need, and do whatever we can to care for them. It occurred to me that maybe it wasn't just the ones in robes he was trying to warn.

I was still trying to decide if I believed he was telling us what God wanted us to hear when he started talking again. And I still remember what he said next,

But one who is more powerful than I will come, the straps of whose
sandals I am not worthy to untie. He will baptize you with the
Holy Spirit and fire. His winnowing fork is in his hand to clear his
threshing floor and to gather the wheat into his barn, but he will burn
up the chaff with unquenchable fire."

Luke 3:16-17 (NIV)

After that, he went back to his baptizing and I started walking back home. I forgot all about the robes. All I kept thinking about were my shirts. And my snacks. Finally, I stopped walking. I took off my outer shirt and handed it to a man who did not have a shirt. Then I reached in my jacket pocket. I took half of my snacks and handed them to a young girl walking with her family. She looked hungry.

I just wanted to tell you about my day yesterday.

Thanks for listening. Amen.

Fourth Sunday of Advent

Luke 1:39-46(46-55)

Redefining "Blessed"

It is one of those great moments that ends up being a song, or a painting. Over the years it becomes a symbol of peace and hope, and everything good. Mary is a young girl whose life has been turned upside down. It might have been for a very good cause, but it still meant that everything in her world had changed, and she was trying to figure out what it all meant.

We aren't told why she made the trip, but at some point, Mary went to the town of Hebron to visit with her aunt Elizabeth, the wife of a priest named Zechariah. The priests of Aaron were one of two families who were descended from a long line of temple priests and took turns performing the routine jobs at the temple in Jerusalem. We believe Elizabeth lived in Hebron, which is south of Jerusalem, and a long way from Mary's home in Nazareth, so we're not sure why Mary made that long and dangerous trip.

But what made this visit so special is the experience described in today's scripture, with words that have become known as the "Magnificat", crafted into music by Vivaldi, Bach, Rachmaninoff, and many others. It is part of daily vespers in the Roman Catholic church, and sections of the passage are a part of most every Christian tradition. They form that image of God being present, of God acting in people's lives, they are a symbol of God's blessing.

The week before the day we remember that baby being born seems to be an appropriate time to talk about God's blessing of Mary, and what it means to receive God's blessing. We think about it a lot.

Have you ever said to someone, "God bless you!" or "Have a blessed day!" or perhaps, something like, "Count your blessings," "It's just a blessing in disguise," or maybe you even told someone,

"You have been a blessing to me."

Have you ever said one of those things? Well, if so, you might want to rethink doing that in the future.

We usually think of God's blessing as something that we might want to sing about and wish for someone else. Maybe God's blessing is something that brings peace, happiness, comfort, good health, a long life, or even success and riches. We sometimes begin to believe that when those good things happen in our lives, God is blessing us. And when the difficult and sometimes painful things happen, it means that God may be punishing us, or even worse, has abandoned us. But if we look at Mary's blessed life, we find that those who promised us that following God would bring you blessings of comfort, riches, peace, happiness, and success, are promising something that God never promised.

Let's take a moment and remember Mary.

We first hear of her when she was about twelve years old. Old enough to be betrothed, but young enough to still be going to the well for the family's water. She was a young girl, living in a very small town of a few dozen families, who found out that she was going to have a child. Mary may have understood her child had come from God, but it was probably more difficult to convince her family, the rest of the little town of Nazareth, and her husband-to-be. In fact, it took another angel to help Joseph understand and accept what had happened.

At some point after that, perhaps because she just needed to get away from the small-town talk, she made the dangerous trip down to visit her aunt. She traveled the hundred-plus miles through the mountains and wilderness on foot. Are you counting her blessings yet?

At some time later, she went back home and we are told that when Herod announced the census a few months later, she and Joseph had to once again make the journey from Nazareth, stopping in Jerusalem. This time, close to the birth of her child, she walked the miles through roads now crowded with other travelers going home for the census — more blessings.

The relatives in Bethlehem had a full house and all of the

guesthouses were full, so Mary was led to a cave behind the house where the animals were kept. She was given fresh straw to sit on. When her baby was born, one of the large, carved stone cattle feeders was moved over so she could put her newborn baby. She spent a good part of her time standing guard over that manger to keep the curious and hungry animals away from her infant son — blessings.

Then there were the shepherds and the men from somewhere in the east. As those groups spread the word, more people came, all wanting to see the baby and remind Mary of how God had blessed her. Oh, and you do remember that one of the gifts those men from the east had brought was the herb commonly used to anoint a body after someone had died? I wonder if that felt like a blessing as Mary held her little boy in her arms.

Then they learned that Herod was determined to kill her baby, and she and Joseph had to sneak out of town in the dark of night and travel hundreds of miles through the desert to find temporary safety in Egypt. Are you feeling blessed yet?

A few months or years later, sometime after Herod was dead, the small family returned through the desert and made their way back to small town Nazareth, where it had all begun. I wonder how that went? Small towns tend to have long memories about some things.

We don't know much about Mary's experience raising her boy, other than the time he ran off and they found him talking with people in the temple. When someone asked him about his father, the boy said that he was standing in his father's house. I imagine that hit daddy Joseph pretty hard, and I'm guessing there may have been similar experiences for Mary. I'm thinking it wasn't all that easy raising the Son of God.

I imagine you are understanding my point about the meaning of "blessing", but we can't stop yet. We need to remember the day Jesus left Mary and Joseph in Nazareth and moved to Galilee to begin his ministry. Mary knew that Nazareth was a safe place, but Galilee was not. She had to know in her heart what was coming.

And we need to remember the day she went to visit him in

Galilee and someone went into the house to tell Jesus that his mother was there. She heard him say, "Who is my mother?" I'm not sure she heard any of the rest of what he said. I don't think I would have.

And we need to skip ahead and remember the evening standing outside the walls of Jerusalem. At the stone quarry, the one the Romans used to crucify criminals. Mary stood there watching.

Of course, we remember that a few days later she stood outside the empty tomb, with everyone telling her that her son had been raised from the dead. I am sure that was good news for Mary. But I still have to wonder.

In my mind, as she stood outside the empty tomb she thought back to that first morning at the well when the angel first told her. And she thought back to the trip to Bethlehem, and to Egypt, and back. And I think she thought about all of those other things and all of the ones we know nothing about. But in my mind, if it were me standing there, I think the biggest memory going through my mind would be that visit with Elizabeth and the time she told me how much God had blessed me and my baby boy.

If it were me standing there outside the tomb, even though I was told my son had been risen from the dead, I would probably still be having second thoughts about the whole idea of being blessed.

Please understand, I am not saying we should not pray for and offer God's blessings. But I am saying that I believe it would be helpful for us to remember just what it does mean to be blessed by God.

The word we say as blessed does not mean "happy", "lucky", or "success" but it comes from a word meaning "holy." Someone who is blessed is someone who is somehow made more God-like.

But there is something even more telling. The original word for "blessed" is also used to describe that which used to be upright and straight, but by some event or events has become bent. To be blessed means to experience something that makes us more God-like, by bending us, by reshaping us into the person God intends us to be.

It is another of God's great surprises.

We come to Christmas thinking that God blesses us by bringing us happiness, joy, health, and wealth. And then Christmas arrives and reminds us, with Mary's help, that being blessed means to become someone different. Someone who understands that:

Being blessed does not mean we always have good things happen, but that God is using us to do good things for others.

Being blessed does not mean we will always be happy, but that God is using us to bring more happiness to others.

Being blessed does not mean we will receive things, but that God is using us to give to others.

Being blessed does not mean we will always be comfortable, but that God is using us to comfort others.

Being blessed does not mean we will live a long and peaceful life, but that God is using us to help others fully live their own lives.

Being blessed does not mean we will have a grand house to live in, but that God is using us to see that others have a home.

Being blessed does not mean that we will have all of the things that we believe happy and successful people will have, but that God is using us to remind those around us to pay no attention to what others have, or look like, or where they come from.

Being blessed this Christmas may not mean getting all of the gifts you would like to receive, or being perfectly healthy and happy, or even getting through the big family day without cousin Henry doing something to irritate aunt Ruth and once again starting the big argument everyone knows is coming. In fact, being blessed by God isn't about us at all. Our being blessed is God's way of making us more God-like; bending us so we can live our lives the way God hopes we will live them to help others.

As I said at the beginning, if I say, "God bless you!", I may not be offering you something you really would care to have. But it is still something I hope for all of us, so I will go ahead and say it.

"May God bless you. May God use you to do great things this week for those who are around you, and may you have a blessed Christmas!" Amen.

"POW!"

Let's remember the story together.

It was a quiet night. We leaned our backs against the tree and tried to relax our aching muscles. It had been another busy day. We started the morning up on the hillside where the grass was deep, but as afternoon came and it got hotter, we led the sheep down into the valley where it was cooler and they could drink from the stream. That's when the young one got caught in the current and we had to pull it out with our shepherd's crook. Again. As the sun started to set, we led them back to the sheepfold, and we stood by the gate as they walked in. We stopped each of our sheep as it got to the gate and we examined it closely for any cuts or scrapes, especially on their soft noses. Some of the stones on the hillside were pretty sharp. Once all of the sheep were safely inside, we walked around the stone wall of the sheepfold to make sure none of the stones had fallen and left a hole where a sheep might escape or something else might get in to harm them. We cut a few new branches from a thorn bush and put them on top of the wall where the old pieces had blown off. That would keep anything from trying to crawl over the wall to get in. But now it was quiet, and we watched the sheep settled safely inside the sheepfold and felt the cool night breeze begin to blow through the valley.

And then, "POW!" The sky lit up. Angels appeared. Sheep started bleating. It all happened so quickly that our first reaction was to curl up on the ground and cover our heads. But we didn't even have time to do it before we heard, "Don't be afraid, we come to bring you good news."

When it was over and the sky was dark again, we went around

and calmed our sheep, and then we all got together under a tree and all started talking at once. "Did you see that? What do you think it meant?" Finally, we drew lots and selected those who stayed to watch the sheep while the rest of us went into town to find the baby the angel had talked about. We were so excited that we told everyone we saw about what had happened. We found the baby and told them what we saw and heard too. And then, we went back to work.

Here is my question for you:

Out of everyone available, why did God pick those guys to tell about the birth of Jesus? Why did the whole thing begin with God announcing it to a bunch of shepherds? Now, there is nothing wrong with shepherds, don't get me wrong. Shepherds are hardworking people. They are honest and trustworthy and spend their time taking care of other people's sheep. But they aren't the kind of people you might expect to be picked for a major announcement from God. They were great with sheep, but they usually weren't all that good with their people-skills. And they spend most of their lives living out somewhere in the hills with animals. You might even remember the old joke that says you can hear most people coming to see you, but you can *smell* the shepherds coming.

Sometimes I wonder what Mary and Joseph thought when they saw a bunch of shepherds show up? I wonder if Joseph tried to keep them out? I wonder if Mary thought, "Good grief, what next? A bunch of foreigners?"

Those shepherds were honest, trustworthy, hardworking people, but it all comes down to a key question: "Who would ever listen to a shepherd?"

It's Marketing 101. When you have a major announcement to make, you make that announcement where the audience is most likely to see and hear it, and have it made by someone who the audience will pay attention to.

Now, a priest, of course. Or, maybe a Pharisee, or a Sadducee. Maybe even a rabbi if they were from a decent size synagogue in a well-known city like Jerusalem, and as long as he taught the proper things. A strong, well-known religious leader would seem to be the ideal person to make this type of announcement from God. Maybe even someone in government leadership? Those are people who can pull an audience and have their message be heard. If one of those people said that God had talked to them, it would certainly get people's attention. But shepherds?

Once again, it is one of God's surprises!

I have been thinking about why God chose shepherds.

What would have happened if the angels had appeared to the Pharisees, or the temple priests, or a government leader? Their immediate response might have been the same shock and surprise the shepherds felt, but it would have soon changed to their asking, "Is this something we can use, or is this a threat to us?" They would have made the trip to Bethlehem, but it would have been an intelligence-gathering mission rather than an act of worship. They most certainly would have told people about what they had heard and seen, but you wonder how they would have spun it to make it say what they wanted it to say to support their positions. They would have been heard for sure, but the chances are good that what God had actually done is not what would have been heard.

But look at what the shepherds did. They heard the news and were humble about it. They made the trip to town to see it and tell people about it. They didn't say, "You need to listen to us because God talked to us instead of anyone else." They said, "We were just sitting out there when, "POW", the sky lit-up, and a bunch of angels flew down and told us to go into town and see a baby because God sent it to be the Lord." And then they went back to work.

People might have been surprised to hear it from shepherds, or honestly, to hear anything at all from shepherds, but what they heard from them was what God had done, not what the shepherds wanted people to think had been done. They had been put in a situation most people believed was over the shepherd's heads, but they did what they knew how to do. They did what God asked them to do.

Every once in a while, we have an experience that feels like God is speaking directly to us. It might be during a conversation with someone who is hurting. It might be when we are struggling with a decision that needs to be made. How are we going to respond? Do we say, "Hey! God talked to me! You all need to follow me, or buy my book, or do whatever I tell you to do. God talked to me and that means I am special." Or, are we just going to do what God asks?

Let me give you an example. I am talking with some people at the coffee shop and someone mentions a friend of ours who has a very sick child. When I hear it, it feels like God speaks directly to me and tells me that I should go to that friend and let them know that they are cared about. Now, I have a choice.

I might go to that friend's house and say, "Bob, God spoke to me. God told me to come here and visit with you. God called me, Bob, to come here to let you know that God cares about you and your family." Or do I go there and say, "Hi Bob, I just heard about your son, I am so sorry. Is there anything at all I can do to help: run to the store for you, take care of the yard, or just buy you a cup of coffee?"

We do not need to be someone special to have God speak to us. We do not need to have some special role, or position, or training for God to be able to use us. When God speaks, all we have to do is be ourselves and do what God asks us to do. Not try to convince anyone that God did speak to us. Not try to make ourselves look important. Not even try to convince other people to believe in God. We do what God asks us to do because God asks us to do it.

And why us? Because we were the one that God asked.

Maybe the shepherds weren't the kind of people anyone would have picked to do God's work, especially for something as big as this. But you know, God never has agreed all that much with what we think about other people. Just look around. Most of the people God has picked to bring about major changes were never people who would have even made our first long list of possible names we would have then whittled-down to the cream of the crop.

There is something about us that makes us want to define other people. We have our categories and labels we use to define them:

How they look.

What they wear.

Where they are from.

Where they live now.

What they do.

Do they have a job?

Do they have the "right kind" of job?

Do they make enough money to take care of themselves?

Just how much money do they have?

Do they believe what we believe?

There are more, and the reality is that those shepherds would have never been selected based on our categories. But the good news is that God doesn't care about our categories. God doesn't care about how we might label people or about how other people might label us.

God calls who God calls because those people will do what they are asked to do.

If and when God speaks to us, our task is not to try and figure out "Why me?" or look for ways to use that as an opportunity. Our task is to simply do what we have been asked to do.

While the usual focus of the Christmas story is on the baby Jesus and the birth of the Son of God, one of the most amazing parts of the Christmas story for me is that God selected those shepherds to receive the good news. One of the greatest moments in history was not announced by powerful religious leaders, powerful politicians, or by anyone else in a role that you would expect to speak for God.

It was quite a surprise. And sometimes, even more surprising and against all odds and human logic, "POW", sometimes God selects us.

Merry Christmas to the shepherds, and to all of us. Amen.

First Sunday after Christmas Day

Luke 2:41-52

Finding The Sermon

We are going to do things a little differently today. Instead of me just preaching you a sermon, we are going to see if we can find the sermon that is hidden inside today's passage of scripture. I think there are a lot of different messages in this story about the young boy Jesus, and maybe we can sort through them and find the one that speaks to us best today.

The story tells us one of the few things we know about Jesus as a young boy. He and his family had gone to Jerusalem to celebrate Passover, something they apparently did every year. When Mary and Joseph started back home, they realized Jesus wasn't with them. They went back to Jerusalem and it took them three days to find him again. When they did finally find him, he was sitting on the steps of the temple, arguing with the religious teachers, and we're told Jesus wasn't all that concerned that his parents had been worrying about him. Finally, it says they all went back home and Jesus behaved just fine after that.

Okay, let's see if we can find our message in there somewhere.

Since we don't know very much at all about Jesus growing up, maybe that is what we can preach about here. While we don't know much about Jesus as a young boy, maybe we could have kind of a history lesson of what other twelve-year-old boys were like in the first century, and do kind of a "maybe it was like this, maybe it was like that" kind of sermon.

Or maybe we could use some of the apocryphal stories we have about Jesus as a child. The word "apocrypha" means "hidden" or "doubtful", because they are more myth than anything that really happened. In fact, your Bible may have the books of the apocrypha in it, with some of those stories that people liked to

38

tell each other but realized they were just stories. Like the story about Jesus out playing in the mud with other children. Some of them started making little birds out of the mud, so Jesus made a bird out of his mud and it got up and flew away. Or the time the little boy Jesus became angry with another child and pointed his finger at him and made him very sick. Maybe we could have a sermon about the dangers of accepting made-up stories and truths for real truths.

Or maybe our sermon could say that the reason we don't know very much about Jesus as a child is because God did not think it was important. What is important is that we remember Jesus's birth, what he did during his ministry, and his death and resurrection. That's why those things are talked about in scripture and the rest isn't. Maybe our sermon could be about how we should spend our time thinking about the things that are really important in life, and not spend our time worrying about the things that aren't.

Or what about this? Jesus' mother and father started for home and didn't even check to see if Jesus was with them. They left their twelve-year-old son behind, and it took them three entire days to find him again. What kind of parenting is that? Maybe that is meaningful sermon material? But then, we recall that Mary was probably only twelve when that angel showed up at the well and remember that a twelve-year-old in the first century was very different from a twelve-year-old in the twenty-first century. But, hey! Maybe our sermon could be about the dangers of reading first-century-scripture through twenty-first-century eyes.

Or here's a good one. When they finally found Jesus in the temple, he was sitting on the teaching steps with the teachers. Those were the big steps on the side of the temple where the teachers sat arguing with their students. Arguing was the form of teaching in the first century. It was not only okay to argue and question, it was required for learners to ask questions and challenge their teachers about what was being taught. They believed that if we learned how to think deeply enough to argue about our thoughts and beliefs, we would be able to make better decisions about how to live our lives. And they found Jesus sitting right there in the middle, arguing with them like he was one of them. Maybe our sermon could be about why so many people are afraid of someone asking questions about their faith today. Our sermon might ask why people, who say they believe that Jesus has once-and-for-all won the battle against evil, are so afraid of so many things?

Or maybe our sermon could be about how difficult parenting can sometimes be. When Mary and Joseph finally found their son, Mary asked him why he had treated them like this and told them how worried they had been about him. Apparently, Jesus just looked up at them and said, "What's the big deal? You should have known I would be here in my Father's house." We are told Mary and Joseph did not understand what he meant, but I have an idea of how dad-Joseph might have felt about it. In my mind, I wonder if Mary pulled her husband aside and said something like, "Now, Joseph, you know he didn't mean it the way it sounded." Parenting any child can be challenging sometimes, so maybe this would be a great opportunity to preach about that.

One of the lines that is interesting to me is the one that says when they finally got back home to Nazareth, Jesus was obedient to them. It just intrigues me why that was said. Had Jesus not been obedient before? Had they had other problems with Jesus paying more attention to God than to them? If so, how did they handle it? That might be really interesting to preach about.

I've heard a lot of sermons preached about the line that says, "His mother treasured all these things in her heart." That was same thing that was written about Mary back in that cave in Bethlehem after the shepherds and wise men had come to visit. Though, I think that first time they said Mary "pondered" those things in her heart. Maybe we could preach about the meaning of "pondered" and "treasured" and see what that might tell us about Mary.

There are a lot of possibilities for sermons from this one passage. Granted, some of them are better than others, and some would be more timely than others, too. But we certainly have a lot of ideas to choose from.

But to tell you the truth, there is one more thing I hear this story saying to me. It isn't actually said in the story, but it is there and it is yelling at me.

It's about the end of the story and everyone being back in Nazareth. Or, I guess it's about the difference between Jesus being in Nazareth and being anyplace else. Nazareth was safe. In Nazareth, the boy Jesus could be the boy Jesus. Sure, everyone knew he was more than that, but day to day he probably just lived his life like the other kids in town. It was during those trips to Jerusalem that things were different. It was one thing to sit and argue with the teacher in the synagogue school in small-town Nazareth. But if you were a twelve-year-old boy sitting on the teaching steps of the temple in Jerusalem, arguing, and winning those arguments, with the leading teachers of the nation, that was altogether different.

In Nazareth, people may have somehow understood Jesus to be the Son of God, but most of the time they just thought of him as Joseph and Mary's boy. Outside of Nazareth, he was a stirrer. He was someone who stood out from the crowd and stirred things up. We aren't told it in the story, but you can be absolutely certain that the temple leaders and the political leaders were very much aware of that twelve-year-old who caused the commotion at Passover. And the one thing those leaders were not about to tolerate was a commotion. We can also be quite sure that when Jesus and his family returned to Jerusalem for Passover every year after that, those leaders had their informants watching him and following every move he made. But back in Nazareth, Jesus was home, and he was safe.

That is the sermon I hear speaking to me. It is about that day when Jesus was older and had just gotten the message that Herod had killed John the Baptist. He knew it was time. It was time to leave Nazareth. It was time to give up the safety of being Joseph and Mary's boy and tend and feed God's sheep in his role as the Son of God.

Regardless of who Jesus was, I do not believe it was an easy

41

step to take. Just like his prayers in Gethsemane before his arrest, in my mind, he stood on the hillside overlooking the Jezreel Valley and he struggled. It was the valley where Gideon had stood against and defeated the Midianites and Amalekites. It was the valley where King Saul had been defeated by the Philistines. At the end of the valley, in the distance, he could see the remains of the old city of Megiddo where King Josiah had fallen against the Egyptians. Nazareth was safe, but it was in the middle of a nation that had stood with God against enemies for as long as anyone could remember. And now it was Jesus' time to stand.

Jesus could have stayed in Nazareth. He could have taken over the family business, had a family, and enjoyed what might have been a nice, long, life. He still could have gone to Jerusalem every year and helped keep things stirred up, and he would probably still be remembered today as a good man who had tried to make a bit of a difference. But he knew that was not who he was supposed to be.

He made the choice.

Jesus chose to leave Nazareth and move to Capernaum on the north shore of the Sea of Galilee, where he would be seen and heard, and he could begin doing the things he had been sent to do. His work would no longer be a once-a-year holiday activity, but it would become his way of life for as long as it would last.

That is the sermon I hear. And I think it is appropriate for the week after Christmas. Christmas is safe. It is joyous. It is about beginnings, and hope, and miracles. But now we begin the journey from Christmas Day to Good Friday, and then to Easter. It ends up being just as joyous and miraculous, but it can be a tough trip getting there. We have a choice to stay here in the safety of a Christmas faith, or to take the steps we need to take to become who God intends us to become.

For me, that means we might think about how God is challenging us to give up some piece of security and stand out from the crowd. Something we might change in our lives that might make it possible for God to use us in ways we are meant to be used. It may be something very simple, not as dramatic as a move from Nazareth to Capernaum. Maybe it's as simple as changing how we treat someone, or how we treat ourselves. Maybe it's as simple as asking someone for help or offering our help to someone else. Maybe it's as simple as saying, "I am sorry" or "I love you."

That's the sermon I hear in this passage today. Whatever life was like for Jesus when he was younger, the day came when he made the choice to become who he was meant to be. Because of that choice, we went from Christmas to Easter morning. He knew who he was, and he knew who God had asked him to become. He made the choice to stand.

And that part of the story makes me hope that I will always do the same. Amen.

Matthew 25:31-46

Seating Arrangements

Jesus and his disciples had spent the day at the temple again. As had happened every time they went to the temple, they were confronted by the temple priests, the Pharisees, the Sadducees, and a lot of others, all wanting to argue and try to make Jesus and all of them look like a bunch of radical losers. On most days, Jesus just dealt with them and then left.

But today, as they had left the temple, Jesus had said that God was going to come back and destroy the temple, as well as all of those people who had been doing the things to mistreat God's people. And he said it was going to happen soon.

Now they were back at the place they were staying on the Mount of Olives. It was one of those increasingly rare moments when they were alone, and the disciples could ask Jesus about things they did not understand. One of them asked, "Tell us, when will this happen, and what will be the sign of your coming and of the end of the age?"

Jesus told them God was the only one who knew when it would happen, but that they would be able to see the signs and clues that it was coming. He said it wasn't important for them to worry about when it was going to happen, but to just make sure they were ready for it when it did happen. Jesus said when God did return, God would take all of the people and divide them into two groups. He would divide them up like you would separate sheep and goats. One group would be put on God's left side, and the other group would be put on God's right side.

The disciples understood exactly what that meant. They all knew that when a king had a dinner or big event, the seat on the king's right side was saved for the most important guest at that event. It was the seat of honor. The left side? Well, the Bible never once mentions the name of anyone sitting on the left side of the king, so it was pretty clear it wasn't a place you wanted to be put.

And then Jesus said, "Then he will say to those on his left, 'Depart from me, you who are cursed, into the eternal fire prepared for the devil and his angels.'"

Those are big words! Powerful words. Scary words. They are words of warning. Sometimes they become dangerous words. Divisive words. Sometimes these are words that are used to build entire movements upon. Movements who see it as their mission to save the souls of those who might not heed them. These words become their focus, the center of every message they have to offer. And sometimes these words become points of pride. Sometimes they become weapons.

While we certainly need to hear these words that Jesus spoke, there is a very real danger that we might get caught up in the picture they create and miss the real question we ought to be asking; The question the disciples asked Jesus when he first said those words to them.

What are we to do? What am I to do if I want to end up on the right side? And Jesus then told them the two things they must do. First, he said,

"Watch out that no one deceives you. For many will come in my name, claiming, 'I am the Messiah,' and will deceive many." vs:

He knew there would be people who would come along and try to convince them how to have the right seat when God returns. They will tell us, "Here is what you must believe and what you must do!" They will teach different procedures and rules that we must follow. They will sell us their books and videos to teach how to be even more safe and secure, and they will entertain us with their promises designed to make us feel special and safe. They will do whatever they can do to convince us they can guarantee us that seat on God's right side, if we follow them. Jesus said we must be careful to not be deceived by those telling what we must do, so God puts us in the right group.

The deceivers use Jesus' words to convince us that if and when a day of judgment comes, God will look at each of us and ask,

What group or denomination did you belong to?

What scriptures did you believe in?

What social issues did you support or not support?

What lifestyle did you live?

But we have to watch out for these deceptions, because Jesus said these are not the things God will consider if and when that day of judgment might come. They are great topics for building empires, but God has no interest in our empires.

Then what is it that we must do?

Jesus told them that this is what God will say when it happens. God will tell them, "You sit where you sit because of how you have treated me. If you treated me well, I put you on my right side. If you treated me poorly, I put you on my left side. It is that simple."

Both groups will then ask the same question. "When did we do that? We don't remember ever meeting you before at all. When did we treat you well or treat you poorly?"

And here are the words we want to hear. God will answer them, "Truly I tell you, whatever you did or did not do for one of the least of these, you did or did not do it for me."

In my imagination, I'm thinking it got really quiet. Both the people in the story and the disciples.

And if they were anything like us, they would then probably start arguing about the phrase 'least of these'. "Who are they? Besides, shouldn't those people really do more for themselves? If we take care of them, aren't we just encouraging them to stay like they are, and not get to work and learn how to earn their own way?"

But I think those people probably understood Jesus' message more quickly than we do because they understood about sheep and goats, and how the shepherd took care of them. That's why Jesus used the analogy of separating sheep and goats in the first place. He knew they would get it.

At the end of every day, the shepherd sits at the gate to the sheepfold and calls each sheep by name as it comes to him. He stops each sheep and holds a cup of cool water for it to take a drink. He checks each sheep for any cuts and scrapes from sharp rocks and sticks, especially the soft areas around the nose and mouth. He anoints those cuts and scrapes with a healing salve, pulls any brambles or stickers out of their wool, and then lets them go inside the safety of the stone walls.

As the animals came to the gate, the shepherd saw his sheep. That's all he saw. The shepherd did not care for some sheep better than he cared for other sheep. To a shepherd, there was no difference between greatest and least when it came to taking care of his sheep. He was the shepherd. They were his sheep. He took care of them. It was that simple.

When I came to you as someone who was hungry… you gave me something to eat.

When I came to you as someone who was thirsty… you gave me something to drink.

When I came to you as someone who was a stranger in the land… you invited me in.

When I came to you as someone who needed clothes… you clothed me.

When I came to you as someone who was sick… you took care of me.

When I came to you as someone who was in prison… you visited me and did not write me off as "lost".

When did we do any of these things?

God said, "When I came to you as one of the least, some of you cared for me and some of you did not. It's that simple."

For me, everything stops right there…

Did you hear it? Did you hear what Jesus said?

Others talk about laws, rules, and divisions. They warn us about what we should believe, how we should behave, what preacher or leader we should follow, who we should associate with, what we should do if we want to be safe when God returns. So many voices, with so many answers. So many deceptions.

Today we are beginning a new year. We think about

opportunity. We think about potential. Many of us will make New Year's resolutions based on things we would like to do, to create, or to become over the next twelve months. But for me, after thinking about this conversation Jesus had with his disciples, I'm going to think a bit differently about my goals and resolutions for this new year.

From what I hear Jesus saying, if the time does come when God returns and gathers all of the people together and puts some on his right side and others on his left, we might want to remember that God is not the one who makes the decision about which side we get to sit on. We make that decision. We are making it now.

So, as I think about the new year, I have to ask myself, "This year, how am I going to respond when I am visited by one of the least of these? What thoughts will go through my head? What will I feel about them? But, most importantly, what will I *do* when it happens?

Will I care for the least of these?

Will I care for God? Amen.

John 1:(1-9), 10-18

Words

We have heard it before, but let's listen to John's version of the Christmas story one more time.

"In the beginning was the Word, and the Word was with God, and the Word was God. He was with God in the beginning. Through him all things were made; without him nothing was made that has been made. In him was life, and that life was the light of all mankind. The light shines in the darkness, and the darkness has not overcome it."

"This is the one I spoke about when I said, 'He who comes after me has gotten ahead of me because he was there before I was.'"

When I hear these words from John's gospel, one thought goes through my mind.

"Huh? What did he say?"

Matthew, Mark, and Luke tell us stories about shepherds, angels, and wise men, and then John says something like, "This is the one who comes after me and has gone ahead of me because he was already there before I was."

What in the world was John doing here? Did he expect anyone to understand what he was saying?

The Greeks did, and that's who John was writing to. Matthew, Mark, and Luke wrote their stories for the Jews and Gentiles from the area, but John wrote his version for a very different audience. The people of Greece prided themselves on being thinkers, scholars, and philosophers. They studied and argued about a wide range of philosophies and religions and were not the least bit interested in stories about shepherds, angels, and visitors from the East.

They didn't use words to tell stories, but to argue philosophical ideas and truths. Logic and truth was what was important, and if John wanted to explain what God had done in the world, he knew he was going to have to use words the Greeks would pay attention to and understand.

We could talk about what John's words meant to the Greeks, and try to make sense of them now but I'm afraid that would end up sounding too much like a theology class, and I'm not sure that is something we really want to do. But I think there is something more important for us to think about right now.

The power of words — John realized it, and that's why he was so careful to use the words he used with his Greek readers. Sometimes we recognize that power too, especially when it comes to words we use about our religion. Have you ever heard someone having that argument about which version of the Bible to use? For many, the only choice is the King James Bible. Why? The words. Much of the writing is really difficult to understand, because almost no one uses "thees", "thous", and "begats", anymore, but those old words just sound more "holy" somehow — more powerful.

And maybe you've heard someone ask, "Why don't we sing the old hymns anymore?" We don't understand a good amount of what we are singing, but they just sound more holy. The words sound more God-like. More powerful.

John reminds us that words are very powerful things. Sometimes we forget just how powerful our words are.

Have you ever seen someone's face come to life when you spoke with them? Maybe you just said, "Hello", or "I'm sorry", or "I hope you are feeling better", but it was like those words reached out to them and changed their entire world. Words can do that; Our words have power.

Have you seen the face of a child when someone smiles at them and says, "You did an awesome job", or "I am so proud of you"? You can see the power of your words in that child.

Or maybe you sat beside someone who was struggling, and you talked about memories and simply let them know you cared. The power of your words made a difference.

But have you ever said something to someone, and the very instant you heard the words come out of your mouth, you realized that you had gone too far? They were just words. But when you spoke them the world changed. You didn't really mean to change things, you were just caught up in the frustration or anger but then it was too late. The words had been spoken and they changed your world.

Have you ever heard yourself speak those words to a spouse or to a friend? Maybe you spoke them to a parent or to your child.

Maybe you even spoke them in humor, as sarcasm. Maybe you looked at your child and said, "You aren't going to amount to anything at all." You rubbed them on the head to show you were just kidding but did not remember that children do not always understand the difference between sarcasm and truth. You didn't intend them to, but your words changed the world of that child. And if you spoke words like that over and over?

Our words have power.

Or, maybe you held your words back and didn't speak them. Maybe you saw your spouse, friend, parent, child, or neighbor was hurting, afraid, feeling guilty, or just lonely. But for some reason, you did not speak the words you thought about saying that might let them know you cared. Maybe you were angry or felt they deserved what they got, but you did not speak. And the world changed.

Maybe you found yourself in the middle of something that you realized was not the right thing to do. Your head was filled with words you could use to say it was wrong, but you did not speak them for whatever reason. Perhaps it was to protect your job or to not risk losing a friend. For some reason, you did not use the power of those words and the world changed.

Or, maybe you just walked past someone and did not speak your words to them. Not because you were angry, or frustrated, but because you didn't feel anything at all when you walked past them. They were too different, too "other", and you walked past them without seeing if a kind word from someone might have made their world better. So, you did not speak and you changed the world.

Our words have power.

But we know that. It is not a new idea. We remember all the way back to when everything started.

"In the beginning when God created the heavens and the earth, the earth was a formless void and darkness covered the face of the deep, while a wind from God swept over the face of the waters. Then God said, "Let there be light"; and there was light."

Genesis 1:1-3

God spoke and the world changed. And ever since, we have talked about the amazing power of God's word. And we look at the words God has spoken to help us try and understand God, and what God expects of us.

We remember God's words with Moses confronting Pharaoh and then giving the commandments. We wonder at the power of those words. Through the stories of the old testament, we hear the power that God's word brought to the world. It has helped us created this picture of God as the God of power, a God of vengeance that will one day come to clean-up the mess we are in and punish those who have created it.

In the first century, the Jewish people believed that God was the God of their people and who demanded that they do God's will.

They believed that if you were not with us, you were against us.

They believed our enemies were a threat and must be identified and stayed away from.

As a result, they expected that God would one day bring vengeance against God's enemies and reward their loyalty to obeying God's word.

John wrote his words to the Greeks, who believed that God was knowing the ultimate truth that must be accepted by all.

They believed that if you are not with us, you are against us.

They believed our enemies are a threat and must be identified and stayed away from.

As a result, they expected that their one truth will one day overcome and destroy their enemies and reward their loyalty to seeking that truth.

In the twenty-first century, many still believe that God is the God of their people who demands that they do God's will.

They believe that if you are not with us, you are against us.

They believe our enemies are a threat and must be identified and stayed away from.

As a result, they expect that God will one day bring vengeance against God's enemies and reward their loyalty to obeying God's word.

Our understanding of God's word creates our expectations of what God is like, what God asks us to do, or what it means to believe in and obey God's word.

Fortunately, God doesn't pay that much attention to our expectations…

What does God expect of us? What is the Word of God? John uses his fancy words to that question once and for all:

"The Word became flesh and walked among us."

If you want to know what the Word of God is, what God's words are and what is expected of us, don't look for angel armies, golden chariots of fire, and some angry vengeance against enemies. And don't spend time looking for philosophical or religious truths and rules, look at Jesus of Nazareth.

God's word may have been spoken as some vengeful power in the past, but now God's Word has become something else; something very real, and it has come to help us understand once and for all what God is, and what God expects.

What is the Word of God?

"Tend and feed my sheep."

How do we follow the Word of God?

"Care for the least of these."

It is that simple.

And just like God's Word coming to us as the man, Jesus, our words become just as real in the lives of those we speak them to, or in the lives of those we refuse to speak them to.

Tend And Feed, Tend And Feed

Let us pray that we use our words to feed and care for each of those God brings to us.

Tend and feed.

Tend and feed. Amen.

Epiphany of the Lord

Matthew 2:1-12

That Moment In Time

It may seem strange that we are a couple of weeks after Christmas and just now hearing the story about one of the most familiar parts of the Christmas story: the visit of the three wise men. If we created a version of the story for a television series, the wise men would have shown up right in the first episode, or second at the very latest. The baby would have been born, the shepherds would have shown up, and before they were out the door the wise men would have walked in. That's often how we think of Christmas. But we actually do not know how soon the wise men showed up and honestly, there are a lot of other things we don't know about them as well.

Let's remember the story the way we often think of it first. When the baby is born or maybe even before he is born, there were three men from somewhere in the east who were looking for him. Some say they were from Persia, but we aren't told that. Some say they were kings, though we aren't told anything about that either. We are told that they came because they had seen a star in the skies and they believed it was the sign of the birth of a new king, so some believe that means they were Parthian priests from Persia who were early believers in the art of astrology. But from other historical writings, we know everyone at that time believed in the coming of some new king, and all believed that there would be a sign, like a star, announcing it.

We don't know much about that star either. Some point out that Halley's Comet made an appearance about that time, while others say there was a very rare time when Jupiter and Venus appeared very close together in the night sky. Some believe it was a new star sent from God and after it guided the wise men,

55

it fell to earth into a well in Bethlehem where it can still be seen by those with a pure heart. But all we really are told is that the men said they "observed his star at its rising and have come to pay homage."

We while we also usually talk about there being three wise men or kings, we aren't told that either. We assume there were three men since they brought three gifts.

What we are told is that this group of men from somewhere in the east saw a star rising and followed it to pay homage to the new king they believed the star was leading them to. We are told that when they arrived in Judea, they did what all foreign visitors were expected to do, and made the mandatory stop in Jerusalem to pay respects to King Herod, just like we would stop at the customs desk today. And we are told that Herod greeted them, and asked that when they found the baby king to please come back and tell him where he was so he could go and pay his homage as well. The men then went to Bethlehem, found the baby, gave their gifts, and left. That is what we are told.

And when did this happen? We aren't told that either. But based on what we are told, it may have been months, or even a year or more before the men actually arrived in Bethlehem. We know that because when Herod finally took steps to find the new king, he sent his thugs to search for all baby boys under two years of age.

I want you to know that I am not trying to destroy a nice Christmas story here. I am not trying to pull the rug out from under the beliefs anyone has about this story. But, what I am trying to do is point out a part of the story that we often don't think about, a part of the story that tells us a lot more about the men who came to Bethlehem than their homeland, their jobs, or their number. I want to think for a moment about that moment when they had seen the baby and they stepped back outside into the street of Bethlehem. I want to think about that moment in time when they had a decision to make. That, for me, is the most powerful part of the entire story of the men from the east.

Imagine it with me. The men say their goodbyes to Mary

and Joseph and whoever else is there. They walk from the cave, through the rest of the house, and step out into the busy street. In my mind, they stop and stand there. They look at each other. None of them speak. They stand in silence but they are all asking the same question:

"What do we do now?"

They know what they are supposed to do. They have a very clear command from Herod the Great himself. They may have been from somewhere 'out east', but you can be absolutely certain they were very familiar with Herod the Great. They had heard the stories of his power. They had heard the stories of what he did when someone did not obey him, and they knew very well how far he could reach to find that person and make them pay for that disobedience.

In my mind, it is an amazing moment in time.

They stand next to their camels until one of them finally says it:

"Which way do we go? What do we do now?"

This is the part of the story that speaks to me and tells me what I really want to know about those men from the east. That "moment in time" when we learn the truth about who those men were. Their decision of what do I believe in, what do I stand for. Do we go tell Herod, or do we move on? Who am I? Who do I want to be?

They knew very well why Herod wanted them to come back and tell them where he could find the newborn king. Wherever they were from and whatever their role was, they were not stupid. They knew Herod the Great. They knew what he did to anyone who threatened him, and someone who people called a newborn king was a pretty big threat. If they went back, the newborn king would die. If they did not go back, it would probably be them. So, what do we do? Which way do we go?

That one moment; we have been there, haven't we?

That moment in time — that instant when a decision needed made — a decision we know is going to impact everything in our lives from that moment on.

She was sitting at her desk, staring at the piece of paper. Her boss had asked her to sign it, but she knew she would be signing a lie. Her boss and colleagues assured her that "everyone does it once in a while," it was the "way things were done", "the way the game was played." If she signed it, it might even mean a promotion but it was a lie. She looked at the paper and asked herself: "What do I do now? Which way do I go? Do I sign it? What do I believe in? What do I stand for? Who am I? Who do I want to be?

He was in the middle of the conversation over lunch when they offered him the deal he had dreamed about. He had hoped something like this might happen, but what they offered was even bigger than he had ever hoped for. It was all his, if he just said yes. And if he agreed to a couple of instances — no, it was all his if he agreed to lie. He asked himself: "What do I do now? Which way do I go? Do I sign it? What do I believe in? What do I stand for? Who am I? Who do I want to be?

They looked at each other across the kitchen table. The room was still electrified from the words they had just yelled at each other. It had been the most brutal argument so far. It had started as just a little disagreement, but the alcohol had taken it places they never thought they would go. They looked at each other and at the empty glasses and bottles that had brought them to this point. They knew it. In the silence, they asked themselves, "What do I do now? Which way do I go? Is it time for help? What do I believe in? What do I stand for? Who am I? Who do I want to be?

We have all been there: that moment. That moment of choice. Let's go back to that moment in time for the visitors from the east.

In my mind, as they stood there in the street they never talked. At one point, they looked at each other, gave each other that shrug that says, "it's obvious", they got on their camels, and they rode away. Instead of going back to Jerusalem or even back home, tradition says they rode as far as Spain, telling people about the miracle they had seen. If we knew the truth, my guess is that if they went to Spain it was primarily to put as much distance between themselves and Herod's goons as they possibly could.

My guess is that they could not go home again and risk Herod's revenge. They had made their choice.

Moments in time can be difficult and have consequences, sometimes big ones. When Herod learned the men had not returned, he took action. Herod was part Jewish and was familiar with the prophecy that a king might one day be born in the village of Bethlehem. That was when he sent his thugs.

We sometimes try to distract from this difficult part of the story by reminding ourselves that Bethlehem was a very small town at that time. When Herod's thugs arrived, there were probably only 25 or thirty male children under the age of two in the entire village. But I don't think that would have been much comfort to those twenty or thirty families.

Those moments in time can be difficult. But they define us. They show us who we are; who we want to be. A moment in time impacts every moment that follows it. In fact, our lives are a steady stream of moments in time. Each decision we make, each person we meet, each action we take — defines us.

Each moment in time says more about who we are and who we want to be than any beliefs we might profess, any social issues we might champion, any amount of money or success we might accomplish.

Because of a moment in time, we have taken a group of unknown men and created an amazing and wonderful story around them. Sometimes I wonder what story we would be telling about them if they had returned to Herod. Would we be calling them *wise*? Would we even talk about them, or even remember them?

There is one more thought that comes to my mind as I think about the men from the east and their moment in time. They each did not have to face that moment alone. They faced the moment together.

I want to remember that. I want to remember it so when I meet someone who is facing one of those moments, whoever they are, I will remember who I am and go sit beside them so they do not have to face that moment alone. Amen.

Luke 3:15-17, 21-22

Learning Our Role

He was standing out in the river. We can envision John standing out there. His clothes were soaked. His long, wet hair hung down across his face and down his back. If we didn't know better, we might think he was someone who had wandered out of the wilderness and was having some kind of breakdown. He was standing there, surrounded by people who had come to see him. They had come from all around the country and there were even people from Sidon and Tyre: foreigners, and not even Jewish foreigners. They had all come to see him standing there in the river, hoping to hear him speak, hoping to stand next to him and be baptized by him. He moved around in the crowd, sometimes talking and sometimes yelling, and sometimes bending over to scoop up a handful of water to pour over someone's head.

I wonder if John knew what was about to happen? I wonder what John was thinking about all these people and about why they were here? I wonder if he was thinking about why he was there? I wonder if, every once in a while, he just stopped and looked around. I wonder if he looked at the crowds and heard what they were saying? Do you think he stopped and looked at his hands and what they were doing then? I wonder what John was thinking?

We don't know a great deal about John the Baptist. We know he was born to Mary's cousin, Elizabeth, and her husband Zechariah, a priest who worked in the temple in Jerusalem. We assume John's early years were at least comfortable and that he was raised to be familiar with the Jewish faith and the role of the temple. We do know that Elizabeth and Zechariah were already older when he was born, and at some point, John was an orphan.

We aren't told what happened to young John after that. But we do know that the orphaned son of a temple priest would usually be taken care of by the community of which his parents had been a part. We also know that, in the world of the temple, family heritage was the most important measures of a person's role. Since John's father and mother were both descendants of Aaron, the brother of Moses, and the very first high priest, young John would most likely be carefully raised to be prepared to follow his father's footsteps and become a temple priest himself.

That is what we would expect to happen. But today, we don't find John standing in the middle of the temple courtyard, but in the middle of the Jordan River with a crowd of temple authorities standing on the shore watching to determine just how much of a threat he really was. Something interesting must have happened, because instead of following the expected path of becoming a temple priest, John ended up being the voice of a movement whose ultimate prayer was the destruction of the Jerusalem temple.

Some believe it was because of the Essenes. The Essenes were a group of Jewish people, possibly a mix of former temple priests and Sadducees who believed the temple had become corrupted. Because of their more conservative beliefs, most of them chose to live apart from the temple and the rest of the Jewish community. They did not believe in offering sacrifices as the temple required. They believed that one day soon, God would return to clean out the corrupt temple and replace it with a new one. Everyone in the Jewish community believed in taking ritual baths to clean their sins, but the Essenes believed in baths, or baptisms, as part of their daily religious activities.

Some Essene communities followed strict dietary rules, limiting their diet to locusts and honey. Some of the more stringent Essene communities did not marry and were known to adopt orphan boys to raise in order to sustain the population of their community. Some believe that John's diet, his speaking against the temple, and his use of baptism meant that, for some reason, young John left the community of the temple and was adopted into this more conservative, anti-temple movement of the Essenes.

There are many other ideas about what John experienced and why he ended up standing in the middle of that river. But honestly, as we remember the story and see John standing out in the water today, I don't think it is all that important just how he got there. He is there.

Something happened in John's life that led him to believe that God wanted something more for people. Something led John to leave the comfort and security of the temple life and spend years living in the wilderness, trying to understand what God wanted him to do. At some point, something led John to come out of the wilderness and start telling others what he believed. And something led people to listen to him and follow him. Something happened to put John in the middle of that river.

If we knew the truth, there were probably several things John experienced through his life that helped bring him here to the river. Everything that had happened helped prepare him to fulfill the role he was fulfilling that day, standing in that river. For me, how he got there isn't all that important or interesting.

Do you know the thing that does really interest me? I would really like to know what John was thinking about right then standing out there in the water. We know some of the things he said, and what he was doing, but I wonder if there was more going through his head than what we are told. I wonder if he was thinking about what I would probably have been thinking about if it was me standing out there in the water.

I have an idea that if it were me out there looking at what was going on around me, I would have been thinking about all that I had been through to get there. I am pretty sure a part of my thinking would have been something like, "I made it! Finally! After all I have been through, I have made it!"

I'm not saying I would be proud and bragging about what I had done and was doing now, or that I would be thinking I was better than everyone else there, or closer to God than they were. But I do think if it were me standing out in that river, I would be taking a moment every now and then to just enjoy the success.

I have to admit, I would probably look at the crowds lining the shore, and the people still filling the roads to get there. I would probably smile inside to think there were that many people coming to see me. And some of those people had been following me for days, wherever I have gone, they have shown-up. Of course, I would have understood it wasn't just me they were coming to see, and that I was simply filling a role God had for me. I know that. But still, after all I had gone through to get there — just look at all of them!

Although I would know I was fulfilling a role that God had given to me to prepare everyone for God's Messiah, a lot of those people believed I was something more than that. Some of them were even asking me if I was the one God was sending — if I am *that Messiah*. And the way they looked at me and hung onto every word I said. I mean, even the big shots from the temple were here to see me.

Now, I realize what I am saying may sound like blasphemy to some, but I don't mean it that way. I just wonder if John felt any of the things I think I might have felt. And let's be honest. If you were the one standing out there in the middle of all that praise and excitement, don't you think some of those thoughts might have crossed your mind too? Don't you think it is possible you might have had some second thoughts about why you were there or who you were supposed to be?

The young man had the dream of starting his business for many years. He had developed a new model for designing learning activities for those who struggled with traditional learning and he had spent the past twenty years demonstrating how well it worked. It was going to be a business with one goal of helping others; helping them become the person they dreamt of becoming. But it would be expensive to create and operate, so he had spent many of those years finding the resources to make it happen. He had sacrificed a lot. He had been laughed at and had doors slammed in his face over and over again.

Until today.

Today he is sitting at a table with a group people. Each of those people has created their own successful businesses and has the resources he needs to make his business a reality. They are sitting there to sign the paperwork giving him the money to make his dream come true. The young man would finally be able to fill the role he had felt was his calling and become the helping person he believed he was supposed to be.

The papers were passed around the table and everyone signed them. The dream had come true. As they all rose from the table, two of the others walked over to shake the young man's hand. One of them said, "Now that you are one of us, you will of course want to change how you dress and how your wife dresses, too." The other person said, "And you will want to be more careful about the people you spend your time with, now that you are one of us."

"Now that you are one of us." The words bounced around inside the young man's mind.

As he tried to sort out his thoughts, a third person took his hand. "Now that you are one of us, of course you will come to the golf outing this Saturday. It is an invitation-only thing, but now that you are one of us, we look forward to seeing you there."

As the day passed, wherever he went there were more people who stopped to talk to him. People who had never stopped in the past. One offered the use of box seats at the ballgame anytime the young man wanted to use them. Another offered a position on the board of her organization, looking forward to having the young man's new ideas to explore. A third simply said, "Now that you are one of us, anytime you need anything, anything at all, you just let me know."

Other people saw and heard the conversations. While many people he had never spent time with were now showing up every day, many of those people who had been a part of his life for the past many years no longer came around. When he approached them, even those he had felt the closest to, they seemed hesitant to talk with him. It was like they believed he was no longer a part of their world. His dream had come true, but it was not quite the dream he had dreamed.

One morning, as he was sitting at the restaurant, one of his successful new friends sat down next to him and said, "We all think it is a wonderful gesture to want to try and do something to help other people. But if you want your business to be as successful as ours are, your primary focus has to be on ensuring profits, finding opportunities for expansion, and diversifying in ways to have a more stable base you can build upon for the long-term. The idea you have is admirable, but the simple reality is, now that you are one of us, you need to rethink who you are and what you are doing."

"Now that you are one of us."

The words haunted the young man. They kept him awake at night and churned his stomach all day. Who am I? Who am I meant to be?

He had spent so much time and had worked so hard to get to this day and become the person he believed he was supposed to be. And now that the day is here, he finds himself wondering if that person was who he really wants to be. He sees the opportunity to be more than he thought he wanted to be. And the recognition, the praise, the acceptance, the people believing he might be something more. It just felt so good.

The young man knew he had a huge decision to make.

Who am I, really?

Who am I meant to be?

It is a huge decision and can be a difficult one. It is difficult to not get caught up in opportunities and become distracted from who we are and who we want to be. Opportunities for recognition, for praise, for acceptance, for anything that feeds our desires, can cause us to lose track of who we are, who we want to become. We can lose track of why we are here.

I sometimes wonder if John had to make that same decision. I wonder if John, even for a moment, became so caught up in all that was happening that he thought about believing what the people said about him? In my mind, I like to think that John did wonder. I like to think he was human enough to be tempted, even for just a moment or two. I like to think that, because it makes it all that much more powerful when he looks at the people asking him to be the person they wanted him to be, and he said,

"I baptize you with water, but one who is more powerful than I will come" (v. 16).

John remembered his role. He remembered who he was, and who he was meant to be. And if John could do that, there is hope for us too.

No matter how certain we might be in our faith, there are times when opportunities appear that offer us things of which we have only dreamed. Things that offer us answers, money, recognition, pleasure, or anything else that might grab our attention. And all we have to do to have those things is to change who we are and who we want to become.

Who are you, really? Who do you want to be? Who am I meant to be? Why role has God asked you to fill? John reminds me that it is easier to answer these questions if I remember that there is one who is more powerful than me if I remember the role that one has asked me to fill.

John reminds me that I am not here to create my following, or my kingdom but to live my life in a way that reminds those around me there is one greater than me. And *that one* has asked me to do one thing: tend and feed my sheep. That is my role. That is who I am. That is who I want to be.

A bit later, when Jesus appeared in the crowd and John baptized him, the story says that God's voice spoke to Jesus from heaven saying, "You are my Son, whom I love; with you I am well pleased.

Between you and me, I think God was very well pleased with John as well. Amen.

Second Sunday after the Epiphany

John 2:1-11

Who Is This Jesus?

Let's begin by remembering the story together.

Jesus was attending a wedding in the village of Cana, about eight miles north of Nazareth. His mother and disciples were there too. At some point, Jesus' mother came to him and told him they had run out of wine. Jesus took some jugs of water and performed his first miracle by turning the water into wine.

That is the quick version of the story, and on its own it creates a lot of questions. The obvious question is why did Jesus do it? Why did he use his powers to do something as mundane as turning water into wine? It seems more like a sideshow magic trick than a miracle from the Son of God.

And while we are asking, why was Jesus at the wedding in Cana anyway? Hadn't John told us that Jesus had just been baptized and had gone north to the Sea of Galilee? Why was he now in the little village of Cana, some fifteen miles west of the Sea of Galilee?

And why was John the only one of the four gospel writers to tell us this story? Matthew, Mark, and Luke didn't say anything at all about Jesus turning water into wine. Why is that?

I think it might help if we take a closer look at what John tells us about that wedding and the rest of what was going on with Jesus.

It is interesting that John was careful to give us a clear, day-by-day schedule of what was happening. We don't find that done in most of the other gospel stories. But John tells us that three days before, Jesus had been with John at the Jordan River where he was baptized. That means Jesus would have been south of the Sea of Galilee, some twenty miles away from Cana. And John told us that when he was baptized, he saw God's Spirit come down to Jesus like a dove, letting them all know that Jesus was the Son of God.

John said that, two days before, the day after he had been baptized, Jesus was still at the Jordan, and that was when John introduced him to Andrew and Simon Peter, who decided to become Jesus' first disciples.

The next day, John said Jesus and his disciples left the Jordan River and went to Galilee, to Bethsaida, the town on the northern shore of the Sea of Galilee where Andrew and Peter lived. That was when he met Philip, who became the next disciple. Philip then told Nathaniel about Jesus, and Nathanael then became a disciple as well. That was then.

This day, Jesus was in Cana of Galilee, 25 miles west of Bethsaida, where he and his disciples, and his mother, had been invited to attend a wedding.

Are you with me so far? It was a busy few days, and John was very careful to try and keep things straight for us. I wonder why?

One of our questions was why Jesus had been invited to the wedding, and why he made the long trip to be there.

Maybe it was because Cana was Nathanael's hometown. But that doesn't explain why Jesus' mother was there. Over the past few days, she had been back in Nazareth, about eight miles south of Cana. If Jesus was there because of his new disciple Nathanael, why was Mary there?

Some believe that they were all there because the bridegroom at the wedding was John the Baptizer himself. We aren't told that, but these folks believe that John made the trip back from the Jordan and everyone had come to celebrate his special day with him.

Some believe the wedding in Cana was for Mary Magdalene and that Jesus and his family knew her, and that's why they were invited to attend. Neither John nor the other gospel writers tell us that, but these people believe they have found other evidence to support their beliefs.

Some people believe that it was not only Mary Magdalene's

wedding taking place that day in Cana of Galilee, but they believe the groom at the wedding was Jesus himself. Again, none of the gospel writers tell us that, but these people believe they have found evidence they believe supports their belief.

There is another possibility, and one that may be a better explanation of why Jesus' mother was there and why she did what she did later. Cana is only eight miles from Nazareth, and many people in those cities were related. Perhaps a more likely explanation for their invitations to the wedding is that it was a wedding of someone from Mary's family. She would be there, of course, and her son would most certainly have been invited, along with those who were now traveling and staying with him. If it was a family wedding, that would provide the additional motivation for Jesus to make the journey back to Cana and not send a note with his regrets.

There is another clue that supports this idea of a family wedding. It helps to remember that a first-century wedding was a big event that took place over many days leading up to the final full day to formally celebrate the marriage of the bride and groom. At some point on this final day of the wedding, Mary came to Jesus and told them they had run out of wine. This gives a good hint that Mary was a part of the wedding itself. Wine was a big part of the celebration during a wedding, and running out of wine would be a major embarrassment to the family hosting the event. So, it may be likely that Mary came to Jesus hoping he could save the family from that type of embarrassment.

The way John told the story it appeared that Mary knew that her son could do something miraculous. We don't know what she might have seen him do over the years growing up as a young boy. There are stories of the child Jesus performing miracles before, but none that had been accepted as true enough to be considered as scripture. From her words, however, it seemed that she believed he could do something to help.

What we do know is that when she told Jesus they were out of wine, he looked at his mother and said, "What concern is that of mine? My hour has not yet come."

Two things interest me in Jesus' response to his mother. First, Jesus said that his hour had not come. His baptism and the heavenly dove announcing him as the Son of God was just three days ago. Everything was happening so fast. When he went to the Jordan River, he was now largely an unknown person, just another guy from Galilee. But people were talking about him. People were beginning to seek him out. As he traveled from Bethsaida to Cana, the crowd following him began to grow. It was happening too quickly. He knew the crowds would get the attention of the religious leaders and of the Romans, and that would lead to a confrontation. He knew what was going to happen, it had to happen, his hour of reckoning would come, but not yet. He had to reach more people before they stopped him. If he did something miraculous now, it was too soon.

The second thing that interests me is the look my imagination puts on Mary's face. Have you ever seen it? That "mother" look that says, "Seriously? That's what you're going to say to me? The woman who carried you around for nine months, who fed you, who cleaned up behind you, who saw that you had a clean robe to wear? That's what you are going to say? I don't think so!" I can see that look, and maybe the wagging finger, as clear as day.

But John said Mary just ignored Jesus' response. That's another effective "mother" move. Jesus said it wasn't his concern and it wasn't his hour and Mary simply turned to a couple of servants standing nearby, said, "Do whatever he tells you to do," and she walked away.

Whatever Jesus felt or looked like, he finally told the servants to take the six, large stone jars sitting against the wall and fill them with water. When they came back with full jars, he told them to scoop some water out of one of the jars and take it to the master of the wedding, the person responsible for pulling off a successful event. The master drank from the cup and immediately handed it to the bridegroom and told him to taste it. The bridegroom was shocked.

They both knew the normal procedure was to serve the best wine at the beginning of the day when everyone could taste the quality. But as the day went on, and the drinking, you would begin serving the cheaper wine, since no one could tell the difference anymore. But the bridegroom said he was surprised that the master had saved the best wine for last. I wonder if the master of the wedding got a better tip for that because John said the only people who knew what really happened were the servants, and they didn't tell anyone.

All of this brings me back to the question of why John told us this story, and none of the other gospel writers did? I think we find the answer by looking at what John wrote after the wedding in Cana of Galilee. John said that after the wedding, Jesus, his disciples, and his mother, went back to the Sea of Galilee, to the town of Capernaum. Maybe the crowds had found him again and in Capernaum, it was still unknown.

John said that after a few days in Capernaum, it was time for Passover, and Jesus and his mother made the trip to celebrate the holiday in Jerusalem as they always did. But this time, there was a larger group going with them. John told us that it was during this Passover that Jesus went to the Jerusalem temple, turned over the tables of the moneychangers charging unfair rates, and poured their money onto the ground. He broke open the crates filled with overpriced sacrificial doves, he picked up a whip, and he drove the sacrificial sheep and cows out of the temple. As he did these things, he told them all to stop making his father's house a marketplace.

Someone asked him what proof he could give that he was really speaking for God. Jesus said, if you destroy this temple, I will rebuild it in three days. No one understood that he was talking about what would happen when they finally destroyed him. But this last story helps us understand why John wrote the things he wrote.

We need to remember that John was writing to the Greeks and the Jewish community outside of Israel, who were being influenced by Greek culture. John's clear schedule of what happened on the first day, and the second day, was written to show that the things happening were a part of a logical sequence, something that was planned, and that made sense because those were things that were important to his Greek-influenced readers.

The Greeks believed in many gods, each one with its unique abilities, powers, and benefits. There was Dionysus, the god of wine and everlasting life. There was Zeus, Nike, Bia, and Zelos, the gods of power. There was Aletheia, the spirit of truth and truthfulness. And there were many more.

For example, Dionysus, the god of wine and everlasting life: followers of Dionysus' cult told stories of times Dionysus had made wine flow from the ground or had made water smell like wine. What better way for John to show the superiority of the true Son of God than to not just make water smell like wine, but to actually turn that water into not just wine, but the best wine available. Who is the God worth following?

John wrote with a different goal and to a different audience than the other gospel writers. That is why he structured his writing around what he saw were the seven signs of Jesus' divinity... the first of which was the sign of Jesus changing water into wine.

As John wrote his book, he presented three very different images of Jesus, each one intended to stand against the collection of gods recognized by the Greeks. As we read John's words, we see those three images of Jesus:

There is the magician/servant who works miracles for us and gives us what we want.

There is the warrior who will lead us into battle against our enemies and make us victorious.

There is the chosen Son of God, the lamb that will be sacrificed to help others.

The Greeks understood that these were all images they had of their own gods and that John was showing them how Jesus was the one greater than them all. But as we look around today, we can see that we do not always understand what John was saying.

We see groups who believe that faith in Christ means God is the Jesus in Cana of Galilee, a God of magic and miracles, a God who will do what we ask, and give us what we want, who will serve those who are true believers.

We see groups who believe that faith in Christ means God is the Jesus in Jerusalem, a God of power who will identify our enemies and lead us into battle to overcome and destroy those enemies.

We see groups who believe that faith in Christ means God asks us to give up our own needs to tend to the needs of others, and asks us to accept the role of the Lamb of God.

That is what I hear John asking us in the story of the wedding in Cana of Galilee. I hear John asking us how we choose to define Jesus.

Is God a magician-servant?

Is God a warrior leader for some righteous cause?

Is God the one showing us how to be the person God wants us to be?

John is asking us what we want Jesus to be. And since our choice will define who we are, what we do on our own and as a church, John is asking us what we want to be.

Do we want to be served?

Do we want to be led into battle?

Do we want to be brought closer to God?

It is our choice to make. Amen.

Going Home —
Part One: Which Me Will It Be?

Things began moving so quickly. First was the baptism at the Jordan River and the day after that, the first disciples began following him. They went to Galilee, where more disciples joined and the crowds began to appear, wanting to hear him speak. The next day, he performed his first public miracle at a wedding in Cana. The next day, he was back at the Sea of Galilee, in Capernaum, resting briefly before making the trip to Jerusalem to celebrate Passover and take a highly visible stand against the corruption of the temple. Then he was back in Capernaum, where he healed the sick, drove out demons, and drew larger and larger crowds and more disciples. A couple of weeks before, he was a relatively unknown man from a small town in the hills. Now, he was being called the Son of God and was being hunted by the people looking for hope and by the authorities looking for ways to stop him.

Today, maybe to get away and rest, or maybe to avoid things moving too fast, Jesus was making the trip from Capernaum back to his hometown of Nazareth. He was going home again.

Before we go there with him, it might help to remind ourselves why Luke was writing this story and who he was writing to. While John was writing to the Greek community, Luke was writing to people who were simply trying to be disciples of Jesus. They were not all in one place. Some were Jewish and some were Gentile, so Luke was trying to write in a way that would connect with multiple audiences. To do that, he focused on telling stories that could be read aloud as people got together to support each other. He wrote stories to inspire them and to give them courage, rather than writing a historic record of events that took place.

As Luke wrote, he seemed to have had two primary goals:

First, to explain who Jesus was and who he became, and what it meant.

Luke's second goal was to explain what it meant to be a disciple of Jesus: who we were, who we have become, and what it meant.

Keeping those things in mind might help us hear what Luke wanted us to understand about the day: after all of the things that have happened, Jesus made the trip back home.

Many of us know what that is like, going back home after being away and experiencing changes in our lives. Maybe you remember that first trip back home from college, and suddenly going from the more independent and self-directed life at school to being asked once again, "Where are you going?" "When will you be home?" "Are you going out looking like that?"

Maybe it was the visit back home after you were married. It wasn't anything really horrible, but there were several times your new life was clearly at odds with the old life those back home remembered.

Even being on your own and just living someplace nearby — you make that first trip back home and you, and those around you, begin to realize that you have become a different person than you used to be. You have changed.

Sometimes it can be difficult to be our self when we go back home, to be our new self when those who we left behind are expecting the old us. They remember how it was, who you were, and they were looking forward to being with that old you again. It will once again be like it was. But it won't be. It can't be.

It's the old story of putting new wine in old wineskins. As wineskins age, they grow stiff and brittle. If you put new wine in them, wine that has not yet fully stopped fermenting, the gasses will build inside until the wineskin bursts from the pressure. It just doesn't work.

The reality is that the changes that have taken place might make the time being together even better than it ever was before.

We have new things to share, more to enjoy. But, sometimes, going back home can be difficult.

Sometimes, it just feels easier to either stay away or go back home and pretend. Pretend to be the person you used to be. Sometimes it can be easier to put on the old clothes, act in the old ways, avoid the possible tensions, and spend the visit playing a role that is no longer who we truly are.

Sometimes, going back home is a hard thing to do.

In my mind, Jesus had to be thinking about that as he traveled the twenty miles from Capernaum to Nazareth. He knew the people back home had to have heard the stories about what he had done in Cana, in Jerusalem, in Capernaum, and all the rest. He was not the same person he was when he left home just a short time ago. How were they going to react when he went back?

We are told that when the sabbath day came, Jesus did as he had always done and went to the Nazareth synagogue. He might have raised a few eyebrows when he opened the scroll and began reading, but it was not unheard of for a visitor with the ability to read the old scrolls to be asked to do so. In my mind, there were more than a few elbow pokes along with smiles saying, "I taught him to read," or something similar.

He read words from the prophet Isaiah, describing the one that God would send and anoint as the Savior of the world, God's own Messiah. These were powerful words — words that brought tears to eyes as they thought about that wonderful blessing that would one day arrive.

Jesus finished reading and closed the scroll.

I wonder if he hesitated.

I wonder if he considered just stopping there, sitting down, and being the Jesus the people here at home remembered him being? I wonder if he thought about playing it safe, and just enjoying a few days, the way it used to be, without the crowds? I wonder if he asked himself, "Who am I going to be here today?"

In my mind, he looked around the room at the familiar faces. He took a deep breath, and he said, "Today this scripture has been fulfilled in your hearing."

He had done it. He had gone back home, not safely as the Jesus everyone remembered, but as the Jesus he had become. Not as the boy who used to run in the streets, climb trees, or create things in his father's shop. He had taken the chance and had come back home as himself.

Our scripture for today leaves us right there. We will continue with the rest of Luke's story next week, but for now, let's remember the visit Jesus made to Nazareth and just how difficult it can sometimes be for each of us to be the person God has called us to be. How much more difficult it can be when we are with those people who knew us before, and who expect us to still be that person.

As disciples of Jesus of Nazareth, we have been called to tend and feed God's sheep — all of God's sheep. That includes each of us here. So as we go through the coming week, tending and feeding God's sheep, let's also keep our eyes open for those times we might be able to help each other find the courage to be the person God has asked us to become.

Luke 4:21-30

Going Home —
Part Two: Then And Now

Before we look at today's passage, it will help if we take the time to remember a couple of old stories:

The first story is about a time when God caused a terrible drought to cover the entire land. King Ahab and his wife Jezebel had built altars to other gods, like Baal, and had been hunting down and killing the prophets of God. The prophet Elijah was hiding in the wilderness when God told him to leave Israel and go to the town of Zarephath, near Sidon, an enemy of Israel. One day while he was there, Elijah saw a widow picking up sticks. He called to her and asked her to bring him a cup of water, and she did. Then he asked her to go make him a small loaf of bread, but the woman said she could not do that. She told him that she had nothing left but a small bit of meal and a small bit of oil, and she was collecting the sticks so she could go back home and cook one last meal for her and her son before they died. Elijah told her to not be afraid. He asked her to go home and bake him a small loaf of bread and bring it back to him. He told her she should then go back home and bake more for her family. He told that if she would do what he asked, the container of meal and the container of oil would never be empty. She trusted him, brought him the bread, and saw that her containers still had meal and oil for her family's food. God came to the aid of the widow from the town of Zarephath, in the land of the enemy, while the people in the land of Israel continued to starve.

The second story is about a time after Ahab's son became king and continued doing many of the same things his father had done. The prophet Elisha was doing God's work, but the king and many others in Israel did not believe in him. There was a man called Naaman, who was the commander of the Aramean army, an enemy of Israel, and he was very sick with leprosy. Naaman's wife had a servant who was from Israel, and one day the servant said that she wished her master could meet God's prophet Elisha so he could be made well again. After telling the king of Aram what the servant had said, Naaman made the trip to Israel to try and meet Elisha.

When they were near to where Elisha was staying, Naaman sent messengers to him to tell him to come and meet with him. Instead of going, Elisha told Naaman's messengers to tell Naaman to just go over to the Jordan River and take seven baths, then he would be healed. Naaman was a powerful man and he became angry that Elisha did not come. But his servants convinced him to at least give the baths a try. When Naaman, commander of the armies of Israel's enemy, came out of the water of the Jordan River after his seventh bath, his leprosy was gone.

Now, let's take a minute to remember what had happened so far in today's story.

Jesus had gone back to visit his hometown of Nazareth. On the sabbath, he went to the synagogue and read from the scroll of prophet Isaiah predicting the coming of the anointed Messiah. When he had finished reading, he said, "Today, this scripture is fulfilled in your hearing." Luke told us that everyone there was amazed. That's where we stopped the last time.

This is what Luke told us happened just a few minutes later.

All the people in the synagogue were furious when they heard this. They got up, drove him out of the town, and took him to the brow of the hill on which the town was built, in order to throw him off the cliff. But he walked right through the crowd and went on his way.

Luke 4:28-30

What happened?

Their first response to Jesus was positive. They got excited. They said things like, "Isn't this Mary and Joseph's boy?" "Isn't this the carpenter's son?" "Aren't his brothers and sisters still here in town with us?" "Where did this man get this wisdom and these deeds of power?"

Then things changed. Why? What changed? One minute they were all feeling amazed about Jesus, and the next moment they wanted to drive him out of town, and Luke said that some in the crowd even wanted to kill him.

What the heck happened?

As the people talked about what Jesus had said, they started saying things like, "It is really amazing because he is one of us, a hometown boy made good. And just think, if he has done all of those things we've heard he's done for people in places like Capernaum, just imagine what amazing things he is going to do for us now that he has come back home!"

Jesus understood what was happening. They believed that Jesus was going to do the things here that he had done in those other places simply because of who they were. Since they had been a part of who Jesus had been, growing up in Nazareth, they believed he would do even more of his miracles here. They didn't have to do anything or believe anything. God would do great things for them because they deserved it, because of where they were and who they were.

That is when Jesus reminded them about Elijah and Elisha. He reminded them that since Elijah and Elisha's own people did not believe in them, God led them to go and work God's wonders with others — with foreigners — with Gentiles.

Jesus was telling them that he had not been called to bring God's power to those who had some past connection or lineage to rely on. He had been called to bring God's power to those who believed in him, who believed he was the one Son of God, the one who God had sent to change the world. He had not been called to bring God's power to people because of who they were, but because of who they had become. Not because they had been a resident of the hometown of Jesus of Nazareth, but because they had become a follower, a disciple of Jesus of Nazareth.

But the people had stopped listening as soon as they heard the part about Gentiles. "What! Gentiles? Where is your loyalty?

That is blasphemy!" It all went downhill from there. Luke said the people were so angry they wanted to throw Jesus off the side of the mountain, but Jesus just ended up leaving town and going on with his work elsewhere.

They were so angry that Jesus had suggested God would care for someone other than them, even someone less than them. They were so caught up in arguing about what they believed it meant, they missed the important point Jesus was making.

We sometimes miss it too. Let's hear what the other gospel writers said about what happened that day and see if we can hear it.

Luke said, "But he walked right through the crowd and went on his way."

Matthew said, "And they took offense at him and he did not do many deeds of power there, because of their unbelief.

Mark said, "And he could do no deed of power there, except he laid his hands on a few sick people and cured them. And he was amazed at their unbelief."

Did you hear the difference there?

Luke said that when the people reacted as they did, Jesus just went away from Nazareth. Matthew said that since the people did not believe, Jesus did some deeds of power, but only a few. But Mark said since the people did not believe, Jesus could not do any deeds of power other than a few simple ones.

Did you hear it that time?

Mark said the reason Jesus did not do more in Nazareth was not because he didn't want to, but it was because he could not do them. He could not do them because the people of Nazareth did not believe in him.

God's power isn't something given because of hometowns, family lineage, where we are from, or because we have a certain role. God's power isn't something given because we belong to the right group, say the right words, or go into battle for the right cause.

God's power is given when people believe.

And what does it mean to believe? It means two things.

It means to believe in who Jesus was and who he is now.

It means to believe in who we were and who we are now.

Belief in God is not something we just talk about, write books about, create empires around, or use to separate the right people from the wrong people. Belief in God is recognizing that following Jesus means we are no longer who we were before. We no longer worry about enemies or about being better than anyone else.

Belief in God is not a badge to wear or the next level in some game that might lead to life everlasting.

Belief in God is no longer worrying about what happens to us.

Belief in God is *doing*, plain and simple.

If you believe in me, you will do what I do.

If you do what I do, you will tend and feed my sheep.

All of my sheep.

Tend and feed.

Tend and feed. Amen.

Fifth Sunday after the Epiphany

Luke 5:1-11

Doing What Matters?

Let's begin with a question. If you met someone who was hurting, who had lost their job, or were maybe afraid of losing their home, or were worried about their children, if you truly wanted to show God's care for that person, what could you do?

While you think about your answer, let's remember the story Luke tells us today.

A lot has happened in a very short time. Jesus was baptized, he began gathering disciples, he performed a miracle at a wedding in Cana, he went to Jerusalem and caused a major disturbance at the temple angering the religious and political authorities, he went back home and realized how much his role has changed; he went to Capernaum and cast out demons and healed the sick. And now we find him near Capernaum, standing by the Sea of Galilee talking with a crowd of people who are hoping to hear a word of hope from God. The crowd is growing so big it is becoming difficult for him to be seen and heard by them all.

Jesus noticed two boats tied up at the shore with the fishermen sitting nearby, mending their empty nets. He walked over, asked one of them if they would be willing to take him out into the lake, away so he could talk to the people. One of the men, we're told it was Simon, agreed to help. Jesus stood in the boat where he could be seen and heard, and talked to the people. When he finished, he noticed Simon's empty nets and asked him to row the boat further out into the deeper water and throw the nets one more time. Simon said to him, "Master, we spent the entire night out here and didn't catch a thing. None of us. We finally gave up and were sitting there talking about having to sell our boats when you came over and asked me to bring you out here."

But for some reason, maybe because he had listened to what Jesus had been saying to the crowds, Simon said, "I'm afraid it's a waste of time, but if you want me to do it, I will give it one more try."

Simon rowed further out into the deeper water and threw his nets over the side of the boat. He watched the nets sink into the water, and then slowly began to pull them back up. He stopped. "It feels like the nets are caught on a rock," he said. He leaned over and looked down into the water and saw the nets almost overflowing with fish. He looked up and saw Jesus smiling at him. He pulled again on the nets that were heavier than he ever remembered them being, but he started to worry the nets were going to break. Simon turned to the shore and yelled for the others to come and help him, and finally, Simon Peter, James, and John pulled in the nets filled with more fish than they had ever caught before. The three men were amazed and fell on their knees afraid of the power they had just seen. Jesus told them to relax, to not be afraid, and told them that from that moment on, they would help him catch people and not fish.

And let's think back to that wedding in Cana of Galilee. Jesus' mother came to him and told him they had run out of wine, and that meant the family hosting the wedding was going to be humiliated in front of everyone there. Remember that Jesus told her it was not his time to be known yet, so instead of doing a miracle, Jesus walked over to the host and said, "I'm so sorry to see what has happened. I will keep you and your family in my prayers." Or maybe he said something like, "I am really sorry to see what has happened but you know, it would not have happened if you had worked a little harder and planned things a little better. Maybe God is trying to teach you something here." Or maybe he said, "I know it is tough, but God is just testing you. Stay strong and know that one day soon God will help you get your reputation back. He did it for Job and I know he will do it for you."

But you know I'm twisting things a bit here. Jesus did say it was not yet his hour to be known, but he still took the big jugs of water and turned them into wine and helped the host avoid the embarrassment of running out. He could have said any of those other things, but wine was what was needed, so wine was what he gave them.

Now, let's go back to that question I asked at the beginning. If you met someone who was hurting, who had lost their job, or were maybe afraid of losing their home, or were worried about their children, if you truly wanted to show God's care for that person, what could you do?

Now, I imagine there are few of us here who have the ability to turn water into wine, and most of us don't know the secrets of where the fish are hiding. But there are many other things we could do if we wanted to care for someone in need. If we are honest with ourselves, there are probably some things we could do that might directly ease at least some of that person's pain.

So, the first question is, what "could" we do to show God's care for that person?

Out of all of the things we might able to do or say, what are the things that might make a difference in the life of that person, right now? There are many things we could do that might make us feel better, but would not change that person's situation in the least. That is not what we are looking for if we want to show God's love for that person. What can we do that will make a difference for them, right now?

And it might not make everything better forever, but perhaps just long enough for that person to know that someone cares, and because of that, there might still be hope. It might help them take another breath and find the courage to throw their nets out one more time.

The second question is, what "should" we do to show God's care for that person?

To answer that, we will need to take the time to get to know a bit about that person, what has brought them to this point, what is most important to them, and what they care about the most. What matters right now? How can I care for them in a way that will mean something in their life?

For example, how do you help the fishermen? Help them catch fish.

If that person lost their job, is afraid of losing their home, or is worried about their children, does it show God's care for them if we say we will pray for them, suggest they be patient, or assure them that God knows what God is doing and will never give us more than we can handle? Is it God's care to remind them they can learn from their mistakes, or to encourage them to try and understand what God is teaching them through their pain?

No.

I am not saying we should not let people know if we are praying for them. But I am saying that we have to be honest with ourselves and answer the question if praying for them is all that we have to offer them. Prayer is wonderful, but sometimes a touch is even better.

God's care might be in providing a meal, sitting and listening, or showing that we value them enough to stop and not just go past them. It could be many things that have meaning and might give a glimpse of hope. Our role, as children of God, is to take the time to find those things that will matter, and then do them.

Sometimes, if we truly want to be of help, we need to take the time to recognize and do something about our own personal feelings. Those personal feelings that lead us to think that the person we see hurting could probably fix the situation themselves if they would just try harder. Those feelings that lead us to think that some people are more worthy of our help than others because of where they are from, or what they have done, or anything else we might use to divide people into categories. Those personal feelings that lead us to think that the person experiencing the pain probably deserves it.

Before we end, let me say that, yes, I do realize there will be times that some people will take advantage of our caring for them. Yes, some people are playing a game and using people like us to their own ends. But not all of them. If we do care enough to take the time to get to know what is going on with that person, it is usually obvious when someone is playing the game and when someone has truly lost all hope. Still, there may be times our caring is taken advantage of but the real danger we face is that we might refuse to care for those in real need to avoid being taken advantage of by the others. Our role is to care. We'll let God sort out the rest.

Let's end by asking the question one more time. If, on your way home today, you met someone who was hurting, who had lost their job, was maybe afraid of losing their home, or was worried about their children, if you truly wanted to show God's care for that person, what could you do?

Jesus asked us to "Tend my sheep. Feed my sheep."

Tend and feed.

Tend and feed. Amen.

Two Lives To Live

The crowds had found him again. Ever since Jesus had moved to Capernaum, more and more people heard about the things he was doing and had come to hear him, to be healed by him, or simply to be near him. Capernaum was not a large town, but was on the north shore of the Sea of Galilee, just south of busy roads following the fertile crescent stretching all the way from Egypt in the south to Mesopotamia in the east. It was the interstate highway system of its day and it carried traffic from every land, with every language, and every culture. As people passed by, they heard the stories of this Jesus, and many of them made the short trip to be a part of the crowd that came to hear Jesus today. So, the hill was covered with people from foreign lands, along with those from down south in Judah, which included the priests, Sadducees, and Pharisees from the Jerusalem temple. There were people from nearby Capernaum and Bethsaida. There were fishermen, farmers, tax collectors, carpenters, bankers, the wealthy, the privileged, all standing on the hillside with the abused, the out of work, the prostitutes, the criminals, the sick, the broken, the untouchables. It was a vast sea of colors and styles of clothing. It was a confusing collection of languages. And they just kept coming.

But as we look across that crowd, we begin to realize that even though it is such an amazing mix of people, we can begin to see that there are actually only two groups of people on that hillside. They were easy to tell apart, but not by their clothing or language. The clues were more subtle. For some, it was the look in their eyes. For others it was their posture, and how they moved as they sought a place to stand in the crowd. For others, it was the way they were being so careful to avoid others and try to set themselves apart. There were just two groups on the hillside that day. And although it was never spoken and nothing was done to place anyone in either group, every person coming to the hillside knew about the two groups and knew very well which group they belonged to.

For example, imagine looking over at the front of the crowd near the water. We could see those priests, Sadducees, and Pharisees from Jerusalem. Standing with them were the others with some level of position or power. I imagine tax collectors, moneylenders, and business leaders mixed in with them. I can imagine some of those wealthy traders and merchants who were traveling the big highway nearby. They stood so confident and securely, wearing their expensive, tailored robes, and other clothing. They were clean, perfumed, and many of them had a servant or two nearby to make sure they were taken care of — and to make sure no one from the other group got too near. They probably had that look on their faces that said they knew who they were, and that they deserved to be in the front row, that they expected to be noticed and given the respect they deserved.

They were not bad people — but they are the group called *us*. And the one thing they are most confident of is that the people God cares most about is *us*.

But as we keep looking around, we can see *them*. That's the other group. They stay further back in the crowd partly because of the stares of the other group, and partly because they have come to believe they are supposed to stay back. I imagine people who were sick, some with scars, as well as crooked arms and legs from breaks that were not tended to properly. I imagine people in rags, some so thin I'm sure they haven't had a decent meal for weeks. I see those who are clean and dressed, but their eyes and posture tell me they are hurting so badly that I believe they see this trip to see Jesus as the one, last effort before they give up entirely. I imagine children running around, many in tatters, many without a bath, not understanding why they were there that morning, yet all of them somehow seeming to know to stay within their group. They seem to know they are *them*. Once in a while, one of the children, in the excitement of the game they were playing, moved too near to one of those in the front and was quickly sent back to their place — back to *them*.

They are *them*, and the one thing they hope to hear is that God cares something about *them* too. Even if just a bit.

As Jesus looked across the crowd, I believe he saw the two groups as well. One standing tall and proud, even defiant. The other bowed, broken, humbled, perhaps even afraid. And Jesus began to speak.

But he did not begin by speaking to the *us* group or to the *them* group. Jesus looked at his disciples and said, "Blessed are you if you are poor, because you will be given the kingdom of God."

The *us* group likely looked confused. Why would God want to reward someone who is poor? The reason they were poor in the first place was because God made them that way. A few in the *us* group probably turned to the person beside them saying, "Did he say what I think he said?"

Then Jesus said, "Blessed are you if you weep, for one day soon God will make you laugh."

Again, both groups were likely confused.

Then Jesus said, "Blessed are you when people hate you, push you away, insult you, and believe that you are evil." Perhaps both groups nodded their heads. The *them* group felt he was talking directly to them. The *us* group felt the same way because they knew there were people who hated them because of what God had given them.

Overall, everyone on the hillside was rather confused, and maybe even feeling a little let down. They had hoped they would hear Jesus say something more, something bigger. *Us* wanted to hear something that patted them on the back, and *them* wanted to hear something that gave them at least a little bit of hope.

Now, let's step away from the hillside for just a moment. I need to admit that I'm going to use my imagination a bit to tell you what happened next. What Jesus said was real, but the part that I am adding is that I believe as Jesus started talking again, this time he was looking directly at *us*, that group in the front row of the crowd. Okay, let's go back to the hillside.

Jesus looked across the crowd again and then turned to face those standing in the front rows. And he said,

But woe to you who are rich,
for you have already received your comfort.
Woe to you who are well fed now,
for you will go hungry.
Woe to you who laugh now,
for you will mourn and weep.
Woe to you when everyone speaks well of you,
for that is how their ancestors treated the false prophets.

Luke 23-26

I just went through that quickly, because I want to explain something before we talk more about it. I think it will help explain why Jesus got the reaction he did.

It is the word 'woe'. For us, that word usually means something sad, or sorrowful, or that is some kind of misery. We say, "Woe is me" when something happens that is unfortunate. But that is not what the word 'woe' meant as Jesus used it. The word we translate as 'woe', comes from a word that means "oh no!", like when someone is facing ruinous trouble. It isn't about sadness, it is about "Whoa boy!" It says, "It's over big time!" or even more bluntly, the word Jesus spoke as 'woe', can simply mean 'doomed'. So, let's hear what he said again, and hear it the way he meant it to be heard.

But those of you who are rich are doomed,
for you have already received your comfort.

Can you see what happened? Did you see how *us* reacted? The statements about being blessed might have been confusing, but this wasn't.

Those of you who are well fed now are doomed,
for you will go hungry.

In my imagination, some of those in the front row glanced at

91

their servants who were holding their picnic basket filled to the brim with food that was to be their lunch.

Those of you who laugh now are doomed,
for you will mourn and weep.

In my mind, Jesus' eyes never left the group in the front row. I imagine he had overheard some of the comments and jokes that had been uttered about *them* on the hillside.

Those of you that everyone speaks well of are doomed,

for that is how their ancestors treated the false prophets.

Just remember that everyone spoke well of those people in the front row. They were spoken well of even if one didn't believe it. Because if you didn't, they had many, many ways to make you pay for any criticism.

Now, can you see the reaction of the two groups? *Us* is growing angrier by the second. Some of them have pushed their servants to clear a path from the front of the crowd and have headed for home, determined to find a way to make this Jesus pay for what he has done. Some in the *them* were heard to mumble an 'Amen!' You tell 'em, Jesus! It's about time somebody told the truth."

This passage that we often read and say, "Isn't that nice?" turns out to be Jesus making a huge, and dangerous, attack on those in the *us* group in the front row. It is Jesus making it very clear that he has not only come to perform miracles for those in need, but to bring the word of God face to face with those who have been misrepresenting and abusing it for so many years. The gloves are off.

But I think there is something else that is important to think about after hearing these words so clearly. Is Jesus really saying that people who are rich, have food, are happy, or who are popular, are doomed? Was he just talking about that *us* group on the hillside that day long ago, or does it have something to say to the *us* who are right here today?

I don't believe Jesus was saying there is anything wrong with having wealth, food, pleasure, and recognition. In fact, the reality is that those things might make it possible for you to do some great things. I believe the question Jesus is asking those who have plenty, is what are you doing with that plenty? Or even more clearly, why do you want that plenty?

I think the best way to explain what I hear Jesus saying is to tell you a little story about a man who had plenty. A few days before Christmas, he visited his pastor and handed him ten, sealed envelopes, each with a name written on the front. The man asked the pastor if he would please deliver the envelopes to each person. He said he would do it himself, but each envelope contained ten, one-thousand-dollar bills, and he did not want the people to know they were from him. He simply wanted to help and did not want the recognition. The pastor delivered the envelopes and was touched by the generosity, and the impact the gifts had on those who received them. He believed it was an act of kindness that served as a warm reminder of the goodness that still does exist in the world.

A few days later, the pastor was sitting in the local restaurant when he overheard the conversation taking place at the table behind him. The man who had given the envelopes was telling someone else what he had done. At one point the man said, "And it was the smartest thing I did all year. Writing off that ten-grand ended up earning me three times that much in tax savings. Next year I think I'll do twenty envelopes. And you know the best part? Half of those people came and spent most of that money in my store, just as I thought they would."

The pastor felt sick in his stomach as he realized that what he had thought had been a warm, act of kindness, was a well-thought-out, deliberate act of using those ten people to further build this man's own wealth.

I don't believe Jesus is saying there is anything wrong with having wealth, food, pleasure, and recognition. But I believe he is asking us what drives us to have that plenty? Is it the dream of being rich? Is it because you enjoy the positions and status that it brings? Is it that you simply want fine things around you? Or do you strive for plenty so you can use it to do more for others? Inside. In your heart. What drives you? What is your goal?

Jesus was not dooming those people because they were wealthy, but because those people saw their wealth, pleasures, and position as something that was for them, for themselves, something they deserved and that made them special. Like the man with the envelopes, even what appear to be gestures of kindness are nothing more than just another scheme to add to their own treasure.

There were two groups on that hillside listening to Jesus. There were those who lived as God asked them to live, and there were those who did not. And the difference had nothing to do with their wealth, or their appearance, or their health, or their nationality, or any of the other things we often think of. We can debate what we believe makes the difference between the two groups as much as we want, but for Jesus, it was very simple.

And I believe it all comes down to what is in our heart.

There are two ways to live our life. We can be driven by a heart that seeks wealth, satisfaction, pleasure, position, and recognition, acting in ways that everything we do somehow is meant to bring something back to us.

Or we can be driven by a heart that seeks to find ways to give something to the poor, feed something to the hungry, wipe the tears of the weeping, and be a friend to the hated and excluded, not because of what it means for us, but because it is what God asks us to do.

There are two ways of living life. One is blessed and the other is doomed.

There are two ways of living life, and we can only live one of them.

Being a follower of Jesus isn't just about what you have or do not have. It is about answering one very simple question: which life are you living?

Tend my sheep. Feed my sheep.

Tend and feed. Tend and feed. Amen.

Seventh Sunday after the Epiphany

Luke 6:27-38

The List

Before we go to the hillside to hear what Jesus has to say to the crowds, I have a question. Do you ever read those little labels on things you buy — those warning labels? Some of them are simply fascinating. Some of them make you stop and wonder just why they have been put there.

For example, I saw a sticker on a wheelbarrow the other day that read, "Not intended for highway use." I have to admit that I stood there for a few moments with a lot of images going through my head.

Or the label on the baby stroller that said, "Remove child before folding." Or the warning label on the carpenter's electric drill that says, "This product not intended for use as a dental drill." Are you like me and just have to wonder what made it necessary for that label? Or maybe the warning on the jet ski that says, "Never use a lit match to check fuel level." Or one of my favorites is the warning label on the bottle of dog medication that reads, "May cause drowsiness. Use care when operating a car."

The reason I am thinking about these is because today's scripture comes with a warning label of its own and before we go back to the hillside, I want you to be aware of the warning that reads, "Hearing and thinking about this passage may lead to feelings of restlessness and loss of sleep." With that said, let's go back to the hillside.

There is one more thing we need to do. I would like you to make a list. It can be just a mental list, you don't need to write it down. And it is important that we all agree that this is your personal list and not something anyone else needs to see. In fact, we all need to agree that it is not okay to try and get someone to tell you their list. It is private. Agreed? Okay, now that I may have you a bit curious, here is what I want you to do. On your list, I want you to put the names of each person you can think of that you hate. And if 'hate' is too strong a word, put the names of those people you do not like, or prefer to avoid. Or think a moment about the times you hear yourself make that little groan inside each time you see a certain person walk into the room, or you see their image on a screen; and put them on your list. There may be some people whose names you don't know, or have never even met, but for some reason they have become list material. Just add them to your list with a brief note, or anything that will remind you of them. Okay, if others come to mind as we continue, just add them as we go. Now, let's go to the hillside.

We remember that the crowd that had come to the hillside to hear Jesus was a wide mix of people. There were people from nearby towns, as well as foreign travelers who had come from the nearby trade route just a few miles to the north. There were poor people and there were rich people. There were people of power, standing in the front of the crowd wearing their robes with their servants nearby, and there were the poor, sick, and powerless, who struggled to find the energy to stand in the rear of the crowd. Jesus has been talking with them, and the last thing he said about woes has really angered those powerful people; you can see it very clearly in their faces. Some of them are so angry they have stormed away.

When the commotion has settled, Jesus gets ready to speak again. And this time he seems to be looking more at the other group, the powerless group, the people who have suffered, and right now are feeling pretty good after hearing Jesus tell those big shots they were doomed. Some are smiling for the first time in a long time, soaking up the warm feeling of, even in a small way, getting even. They are waiting to hear Jesus hit them again.

And then Jesus speaks to them. I'll paraphrase it just a bit.

"To those of you of who are still listening, I say this: you need to love your enemies and be good to those who hate you. Say a prayer for those who curse you and mistreat you. If someone slaps you on one cheek, don't get angry or hit them back, but stay calm and do not let them cause you to do them harm. If someone takes your coat, offer to give them your shirt too. If someone asks you for help, give them help, no matter who they are. And if anyone takes something that belongs to you, don't let them make you angry and do harm, but just let them have it. Remember, think about how you want other people to treat you, and be sure that you treat them that same way."

Now, let's step back a second. Can you see the faces? They were expecting either another attack aimed at those people in the robes, or at least some words of praise for those of who have suffered so much. They look confused. We can hear, "What's this? Love them? *Them*? You don't mean *them*? You can't be serious. Not that group over there that was in the big cart that passed me on the way here this morning and almost ran over me. They made me jump into the ditch and didn't even care. You can't be talking about them. Pray for them? Be serious."

Before we continue, take a quick glance at that list you are creating.

Then Jesus continued, and again, I'll paraphrase just a bit.

"If you love those people who love you, what credit should you get for that? Even sinners love the people who love them. And if you do good things to those people who do good things to you, what credit should you get for that? Even sinners do that. And if you only lend something to someone you know is going to pay you back with interest, what credit should you get for that? Even sinners lend to sinners, expecting to be repaid in full. But I'll say it again. Love your enemies. Do good to them and lend to them without expecting to get anything back. If you do that your reward will be great, and you will be a child of God. Because remember, God is kind to the ungrateful and wicked, and you are to be merciful, just as God is merciful."

Can you hear the reaction?

"You have got to be kidding me. This all sounds very nice but it just isn't reality. What kind of fool would lend money and not expect to be paid back? And how big of an idiot would I be if someone hits me on the cheek, and I just stand there and let them do it again? You see, this is where Jesus just makes no sense at all. Okay, I understand the part about praying for them, or even doing my best to be nice to them when they are around. But there has to be a limit somewhere."

To be honest, I'm not sure if I'm hearing those things said from the hillside or from here with us this morning. But they are fair words, and fair feelings. Is Jesus serious about this? There have to be limits to how much we take, don't there?

Yes, there are limits to what we take. And let me be clear, because I have heard this passage be used to tell people living in abusive situations that they need to stay in those situations. It may be a family relationship, or even a relationship at work, but I have heard people tell someone they should stay in that situation and, "Pray the abuser to goodness." That is not what Jesus is saying here. Be very clear: Jesus is not suggesting that someone who is being abused or mistreated should stay one more moment in that situation.

There will be times that we have to act, but the question is: how do we act? We do it not by trying to repay hurt with hurt but by separating ourselves from those doing the hurting. We leave. We escape. We do not allow the other person to control how we react and allow them to convince us to become like they are. We walk away. Is it easy? Absolutely not. But it allows us stay in control of our own life and be the kind of person we believe we want to be, and not become what someone else wants us to be. It may take finding help. It will certainly take courage and faith. But never misunderstand and believe that God wants anyone to remain in an abusive situation. Sometimes, as foolish as it may sound, the greatest act of love may be to walk away.

This might be another moment for you to take another quick look at your list.

I imagine the crowd on the hillside had the same thoughts some of us may be having right now, and I imagine Jesus knew that. So he explained that it was very important that they be careful to not judge others, or condemn others, but to make

98

sure to forgive those others. He said that was most important because the reality is that we get what we give. In our modern understanding, I wonder if he might have said it is important because what we do now, is what defines the person we will be. If we spend our time hating and using others, even if we believe those others deserve it, we will become no more than a hater and user. If we spend our time judging others and dividing people into categories, we will become nothing more than a judge and divider. But if we spend our time, even when it goes against everything in our mind, forgiving, loving, and caring for others, we will be doing what God asks us to do and will become a child of God.

But remember that forgiving and loving does not mean that we need to play the fool and ignore what someone may be doing. It means that we must remember to look at that person and remember that they are more than the behaviors you are seeing. Whatever may have happened to them, whatever may be broken, whatever may be causing them to believe they must act as they are acting, beneath those things lives a piece of God's creation that was meant to be something more than what you see today. We do not ignore their words and behavior, and we do not have to live with them, but we try very hard to see the life that is living somewhere underneath, perhaps beaten down, perhaps terrified, and that seed of a new way of living is what we care about, what we try to be kind to, and what we pray about.

On your list, somewhere underneath the things that have led you to put a name there, can you catch a glimpse of that seed of the life God intended for that person? Can you try to focus on that seed and let that guide your caring for that person? And remember that we are not responsible for changing them. That is something that remains in God's hands. Our responsibility is to care for them, and live our lives in a way that will show all of those around us a different way of treating others, and a different way of responding when we are mistreated by others.

It is difficult; the list. Let it speak to you, and make you feel restless, and wake you up in the middle of the night. Let it haunt you and keep reminding you that the ultimate goal for us is to not have that list at all. To not judge between friend and enemy, us and them.

Because the only reason to judge anything is to separate things, to divide things. And God has called us to unite things, to bring people together, to tend and feed his sheep.

Tend and feed. Amen.

Transfiguration Sunday
Luke 9:28-36, (37-43a)

When Following Is Not Enough

The crowds had been coming constantly. A lot had happened since the day Jesus spoke to the group on the hillside by the sea. His reputation had grown, and he knew that meant that his time was growing shorter. So Jesus got Peter, James, and John, three of his first disciples, and as they had done several times before, he led them out to a place away from everyone where they could be alone and pray. In the past, they had gone up north to Caesarea, and they had taken shorter trips into the wilderness to the east. This time, we see them walking up the shepherd trails on side of a mountain. They got to the top, and I imagine they might have just stood there for a few moments taking in the view, and then began to pray.

At some point, something happened. The disciples were exhausted from the hike up the mountain and wanted to sleep. But as they sat down, they noticed that Jesus' appearance began to change. It was like a bright ray of sunlight struck him, almost making it look like he was glowing. Then the disciples noticed he was talking with two other people who had suddenly appeared. As they listened, they began to realize the two men were Moses and Elijah, and they were talking with Jesus about what was about to happen when he went to Jerusalem, and what it would all mean. The disciples were amazed, and as the conversation was ending, Peter couldn't hold it in any longer. He said, "Lord, this is just amazing. Why don't I build three shelters here; one for you, one for Moses, and one for Elijah, so we can all just stay here, and not go back down, at least for a while?

As soon as Peter said it, the ray of light disappeared, and a dark cloud rolled across the sky and covered the mountain in darkness. Then they heard a voice from somewhere in the darkness that said, "This is my Son, my chosen; listen to him." When the cloud moved away, it was just the four of them standing on the mountain top. As they followed Jesus back down the shepherd trail, no one spoke.

Have you ever had one of those experiences; one of those we call the 'mountain-top' experiences? It might have been something relatively common, like that moment you first held your newborn child. Or maybe you have had an experience that was out of the ordinary, but an experience that gave you the clear sense that God was real, that God was there. It may have even been a painful experience, but one that somehow made you aware that you were not going through that experience alone. Many of us have had that experience, some have had several. They are wonderful things, those mountain-top experiences. But they are also very dangerous things. They can confuse us. And they can distract us from being and doing what we are called to be and do.

I have met people who seem to collect mountaintop experiences. They tell story after story of the times they have felt or even seen God in action. They go through the day looking for that next mountain top, looking for the signs of wonder that might mean God is near. As they do, they begin to overlook the darker places where those around them may be hiding in fear, hoping someone might be God's hand reaching out to them.

Sometimes as we worship, we spend time wondering what we might do to make our worship experiences more like mountain tops, doing things that will give people that sense of awe, that warm feeling that God might be in this place. There is nothing wrong with that. Not unless our search for 'awe' becomes more important than our desire to simply care for the people around us who feel no 'awe' in their life today.

Sometimes, those mountaintop experiences can distract us. For example, in today's story, we might get all caught-up like so many others in trying to figure out just where this amazing transfiguration experience took place. People have spent lives doing that. Many say Jesus took his disciples to the top of Mount Tabor, in the Jezreel Valley. They say it would be Jesus' choice since it was near to Nazareth and he had probably gone there as a young boy. Others argue that he led them to the top of Mount Herman, many miles to the north. They say that something this important had to happen on the highest mountain, and that means it has to be Mount Herman, looming in the northern horizon. There are others as well, each with their rationales, and each consuming days, months, and years of energy and study.

And each one distracting us from what is important about that day on the mountain top, and about what is important in each and every mountain top experience we might have. Because where it happens is not important. How many times it happens, and who experiences the most of them is not important. Those are distractions. A mountain top experience can be a very real thing, but it does not happen to simply give us a feeling of awe, or even of wonder. It is not just about a feeling. The voice that spoke from the darkness that day did not say that Jesus was God's chosen Son, and they should all feel amazed about it. The voice said that Jesus was God's chosen Son, and they should listen to him. The experience on that mountain top was not meant to make the three disciples feel anything at all. It was meant to remind them, they are called to listen to what Jesus has been telling them and to do what he has told them to do.

But, like us, Peter, James, and John were distracted.

The very next morning back in Capernaum, as the crowd came to Jesus, a man stepped out and began yelling. He cried that his son was suffering from painful seizures that would cause him to fall to the ground and lose all control, screaming and foaming at the mouth, until the small child is left lying on the ground exhausted and confused. The man said that he had brought his son to Jesus' disciples and asked them to heal the boy, but they could not do it. The man begged for Jesus to please heal his son.

Jesus paused. In my mind, he looked at his disciples, most likely directly at Peter, James, and John and he said, "How much longer do I have to put up with you? You faithless and distracted generation! How much longer do I have to bear this?" Then Jesus saw the young boy begin to have another seizure. Jesus spoke a word, and the boy was quiet. With a word, Jesus healed the young child and gave him back to his father whole and healthy.

And we are told that everyone there was amazed.

That's when Jesus took the disciples away from the crowd and said, "Now, let this sink in this time, okay? Because I am about to be betrayed and handed over into their hands." But we are told they did not understand what he meant, and they were too afraid to ask him to explain. Some believe they were made to be confused, but I have to wonder if the reality was that they were just distracted? Jesus was talking about dark things, and they were focused on bright and shiny things. Things of awe. They even ended up getting into an argument right then and there, about which one of them was the best disciple. I have to wonder if that started when one of the three said something about their little trip up the mountain yesterday.

They just didn't understand.

Why couldn't they cast out the demon that was causing that young child to suffer? Three of them had just stood on a mountain top alongside Moses and Elijah, and yet they could not end the suffering of one small boy? Why not?

Because they did not believe what Jesus told them.

Oh, they believed in the bright, glowing lights, the two men who magically appeared, the cloud, and the voice. They believed in the feeling of amazement and awe of healing the young boy, and of all of the other miracles they had seen Jesus do. They believed in how wonderful it is to be on the mountain top, and how even more wonderful it might be if we could just build houses up there and stay on those mountaintops. How wonderful it would be if we never had to come back down to where there might be darkness, sickness, loneliness, and fear. How wonderful it is to feel that warm fuzziness of God and not have to actually be God to someone in need. They believed in a warm and fuzzy, mountaintop, Jesus, but not the chosen Son of God Jesus who had been telling them what it really took to follow him.

They were not ignorant men, and they were not bad men. They had left their homes and families to follow him, to travel with him, and to listen to what he was teaching. They had given up everything and had followed. But the reality is, following is not enough.

That is the danger of the mountaintop. We believe that if we follow Jesus, he will lead us to more of those amazing moments. Not only now, but how much more amazing will it be when he returns and the sky opens up and... well, you know that mountaintop story, perhaps the most dangerous one of all. You see, if we follow Jesus because of these stories, we begin to believe that all we have to do is be a follower, and keep our noses clean, and that one of these days we will have our little house on the mountaintop where we can stay forever.

But that is not what Jesus said.

If you believe in me, you will do what I ask you to do. You will do what I do.

You will tend my sheep. You will feed my sheep.

Not just the sheep standing in the sunlight on the mountain- all of my sheep. Even those caught in the brambles and briars, those who have fallen into the dark canyons, even those who have wandered away and are lost, again — all of my sheep.

If you believe in me, you will come down from the mountain top and tend and feed my sheep.

Tend and feed.

Tend and feed. Amen.

Eighth Sunday after the Epiphany

Luke 6:39-49

God's Algorithm

Today's passage reminds us of the day the crowds had gathered to see Jesus, and he stood on the hillside and told them all the story of the three little pigs and the big bad wolf. He started by telling them about the pig who built his house out of… no… no, I'm sorry. That was kind of a cheap trick just to try and get your attention. Jesus did not tell them about the three little pigs. But he did tell them some very simple stories that were just as easy to remember, and to some people, that was just as bad as him telling them fairy tales and nursery rhymes.

The Pharisees spent their lives studying the old laws. They had compiled libraries filled with stacks of scrolls, specifying all of the little legal details of what was required for someone to live a godly life. And, they detailed the many different penalties that had to be paid when one of those details was not followed. When Jesus spoke to people using those parables, the simple little stories that stuck in his listener's minds and made God's expectations appear to be so very clear, the Pharisees were horrified. How could he dare take the formal and complex details of the laws of God, and turn them into picture stories like the ones you tell the children at bedtime? It was nothing less than blasphemy, and the man could not be allowed to continue corrupting the minds of the people.

But instead of retelling the people words they would find in the old scrolls of Leviticus, or Numbers, those old rules and laws the Pharisees held so highly, Jesus told them that there were once two men who built houses. One of them built the foundation of his house in a hurry. He didn't take the time to dig deep into the ground and set a good footing, but just set the foundation stones on top of the ground and began building on top of them. He smiled as he looked at his neighbor and saw how much further behind he was in his work. That neighbor was still digging holes, and not a foundation stone had been placed.

A few days later, while his neighbor was just placing the first planks across his foundation, the first builder fired-up his charcoal grill on his new patio and made sure the smoke from the meat made its way into the neighbor's yard.

It was two weeks later that the neighbor finally finished building his house. It was two weeks and one day later that the storm came. You know the rest. You know what rushing water can do to stones lying on top of the ground, and why it was always the better move to set them all the way down onto the bedrock to be prepared for the storms that will surely come. We know that, and the people on the hillside knew that. They could see it as clearly as if they were there when the waters came rushing across the yards.

They understood what Jesus meant.

He told them about the two men walking down the road, one leading the other by the hand. He told them that the man being led by the hand was blind. Then he told them that the man who was leading him was also blind. They immediately saw it. They understood. How helpful was it for a blind man to be led around by another blind man? Where would they go? What would they run into? They saw it happening as clear as day.

They understood.

Jesus asked them if any of them had ever known someone who had gotten a piece of sawdust caught in their eye and they tried to help them get it out. Most of the group nodded their heads. He asked them how easy it would be to help take that speck out of that person's eye if they had a two by four sticking out of their own eye? In my imagination, some of them winced when they saw that image in their mind, partly because of the idea of having a board in their eye, and partly because they understood what he meant and it hit a bit close to home.

They understood.

And he asked them how many of them had grown fruit trees. Many of them nodded. He asked if they had ever ended up with a bad tree that bore fruit that was not good enough to eat. They nodded again. Then he asked them if, every year, they went back to those bad trees expecting to pick good fruit from it? They laughed. They could see the trees. 'Of course not,' they said, 'we would have cut those trees down and burned them.'

They understood.

Today's passage says that after Jesus told the people these stories, he then took a moment to go back and explain what they meant. But my guess is that they already understood. The images they held in their minds were clear.

Build your life on a solid foundation. Follow the one who knows where you need to go and is able to lead you there. Clean up your own life before you attempt to help others with theirs. Be like the tree that produces good fruit.

The stacks of scrolls filled with details and penalties were all summed-up in the collection of images floating in the minds of those people on the hillside. But instead of needing a Pharisee to interpret them, they were perfectly clear.

Parables are a wonderful thing. Sometimes I wonder what kind of parable Jesus might tell if he was standing in front of us on a hillside today.

Maybe he would tell us about the person that has the faulty GPS system in their car that keeps malfunctioning. Somehow it either keeps losing its signal or just gets confused and ends up taking them places they hadn't planned on visiting. Many of us here would nod our heads, just like some already have. Maybe you have ended up in the middle of a beanfield, or at a dead-end next to a lake, or got to your destination and learned that you drove an extra 37 miles because your GPS didn't seem to know about that short-cut everyone always takes.

We understand about following things that don't always know the best way to get where we need to be.

Maybe Jesus would say something the techie folks would relate to. Maybe he would tell us about the person who relies on the algorithm her computer uses to give her the information she needs to do the work she needs to do but there is a bug somewhere in the code of that algorithm. And she knows about the bug but she still continues to rely on and trust what that little program decides she needs to know and does not need to know. Those here who understand things like algorithms might be shaking their heads because they understand.

It seems that Jesus liked telling parables, and he told many of them. And when I come across those times he does, I often wonder why he does it. Why does he tell the parables he tells, and why now? As I think about today's collection of picture-stories, I keep coming back to two reasons I think Jesus may have had in his mind. Maybe you see them too.

First, I think Jesus was reminding those people that we have to remember that as one of his followers, others will be watching us. Some will be against us, but many of those people will be watching us see how to be a disciple themselves. So we need to remember to show them how to build a strong foundation and follow those who can take us where we need to go, and produce good fruit, and make sure we aren't doing things that stick out like a two-by-four, that make it clear we are not actually who we say we are. The truth is that while you will never know who most of them were, as you live your life, you are going to teach many other people how to live their own lives. Jesus is reminding us to remember that truth.

But second, I think Jesus is also telling us that we need to pay attention to who we may be following and be sure of where they are leading us. Pay attention to whatever signals or algorithms we are using to help guide us and make our choices as we are living our lives. As we all know, we live in a day when algorithms have tremendous power. They watch us constantly. They watch what we do, where we go, what we purchase, how much we sleep, what we eat, what we throw away, and what we write and say. Then they use their formulas to make decisions for us about what to buy, when to go to bed, who to talk to, what news to read, all intended, we are assured, to save us time and improve our lives.

I have nothing against algorithms and am not suggesting they are something bad. But I am simply hearing Jesus reminding us to remember that a disciple of Jesus Christ is more than a collection of results from a complex algorithm. Being a disciple is not a complex thing. It comes down to a very simple and clear choice and does not require a great deal of tracking or processing.

Are you showing those unknown people who are watching you what it means to take care of those around you? Take care of all of those around you?

It isn't complex and it is not hard to remember. It's as simple as the picture of the shepherd sitting at the gate as his sheep come into the stone sheepfold for the night. He stops each one and calls it by name as he holds a cup of cool water for it to drink. He removes any burrs or thorns and covers any scratches or cuts with a soothing balm. Then he gives them food, closes the gate to keep them safe and spends the night watching over them as they sleep.

Can you see the picture?

That is a disciple.

That is God's algorithm.

Tend and feed.

Tend and feed. Amen.

Luke 7:1-10

A Slap In The Face

Sometimes it just feels like God expects too much. Have you ever had that feeling? I have. I was thinking about some of those times as I read the story in today's passage from Luke. I mean, it is a wonderful story, and a great example of everything that Jesus was teaching the crowds that came to meet him. And as I read and remember the story I start to feel hopeful and start to smile, and then... and then I feel this tension start to grow inside. It's difficult to explain. It's not anger. It's not fear. It's some feeling of "Really? That's what you want me to do?"

And those are the moments I wonder, "Can I really do this? Can I really be the person God is asking me to be? Can I truly tend and feed God's sheep?"

Maybe it will help me explain it if we remember the story together and as we hear the story, I want you to keep an eye on one person in the crowd. In fact, it is one of the disciples. His name was Simon. Not Simon Peter, but the other Simon. He was the one standing near the back of the group, watching the crowd Jesus was talking to. The other disciples were watching and listening to Jesus, but Simon was watching the crowd. You can imagine him standing there, his eyes slowly scanning back and forth, looking at faces — watching. Simon had been following Jesus and was trying to learn to be who Jesus was asking him to be. But Simon felt a tension inside. So while he listened to what Jesus was saying to the people, he watched.

Luke began by telling us they were back in Capernaum, the town on the northern shore of the Sea of Galilee where Jesus spent much of his time after he left Nazareth. Capernaum was not a huge city, but a decent-sized town, large enough to have its own synagogue. It was a mixed community, not entirely Jewish like Nazareth, but a place where Jews and non-Jews lived and did business together. People still had their individual beliefs but they chose to allow for those differences and still be a community. Maybe that's why Jesus went there in the first place. They were a small example of what he was trying to teach. Capernaum was kind of like what you experience when you visit a place like Epcot at Disney World. You walk along and turn a corner and say, "Well, this must be what it's like to be in Japan!" Capernaum was something like a demo model of what it might be like to live as Jesus had been describing.

A good example of that was the man Luke told us about in today's story. Luke said that one of the people living in Capernaum was not only a Gentile but was a Roman citizen. Even more, he was a military man; a centurion. Any place else, he would be seen as the enemy, plain and simple and the idea of doing business with him, let alone having him as a neighbor, would be beyond comprehension. Rome was the enemy. Rome was the oppressor. Rome represented everything that stood against God and God's people. And a Roman centurion? With that bright red uniform, the shield, and the sword? No, not a neighbor, but an enemy — always and forever.

But Luke told us it was different in Capernaum. And when the group of elders from the synagogue approached Jesus with a message from the man, they began by explaining that, even though he was a Roman, was a good man. They said he had been a great help in building and caring for the synagogue and was someone worthy of Jesus taking a moment to hear his message. Jesus agreed.

There, did you see him? Simon, I mean. Did you see him? Did you see how he tensed-up when he heard they were talking about a Roman? About a centurion? Did you notice how he began moving up a bit in the group so he could hear what the elders were saying to Jesus?

The message the elders carried said that the Roman had a servant who had been with him for many years, and was now very sick, perhaps dying. The message asked if Jesus would be willing to come to the man's house and heal the servant. Luke told us that Jesus started following the elders through the streets to the man's house.

Can you imagine seeing Simon? There he was, walking right there, close behind Jesus. He was watching.

As they turned the last corner, some friends of the centurion came out of the house and approached the group.

Watch Simon.

The friends walked up to Jesus and told him that the Roman did not want to bother Jesus because he knew there were many others who deserve his attention far more than he did. The centurion's friends explained that, since he was a man who understood authority, he knew that all Jesus needed to do was say the words, and whatever was causing his servant to suffer would have to obey and leave his servant in peace. Don't worry about coming the rest of the way, but just say the word and it will be done.

What happened next was where I begin to feel my tension growing inside.

Jesus stopped and looked at the friends who had brought the message.

Simon moved closer to Jesus. Simon was alert. He was braced. His muscles were tensed. They had been brought to this place by a Roman centurion and then they had been stopped right out in the middle of the street, in the open, with little or no defense from any of those who wanted Jesus arrested. It might have been more centurions. It might be thugs sent by the temple. But Simon had no doubt they were there, behind that house, behind that wall, they were there. Somewhere.

Simon was a disciple of Jesus, but he was also a zealot. A member of a group of radical Jews who saw it as their duty to God to fight against Rome — to fight to the death. And there was only one Rome. There were not enemy Romans and neighbor Romans. There were only Romans. Simon had not been fooled. Any Roman who did things in the community like helping care for a synagogue was doing it for one simple reason. He was setting them up for that day when the other Romans would come and take them all away. Simon's right hand was inside his robe, gripping the handle of the small sword that every zealot carried, ready to end the life of a Roman — any Roman. It made no difference. A Roman was a Roman, and would always and forever be a Roman, the enemy of God.

The message was: "Just say the word, and it will be done."

Luke told us that Jesus was amazed. In my mind, Jesus looked around at all of the people who were standing with him in that street. There were people from Capernaum he had gotten to know since coming to town. There were the crowds of people who had come there for the first time today to hear him teach. There were the friends of the Roman. There were Jesus' disciples who had spent the past many months with him listening and watching. And there was Simon.

In my mind, Jesus looked around at them all and then gazed ahead toward the house of the man he had not ever met; the Roman — the centurion. And Jesus said, "I tell you, in all of Israel I have never met a man who has such faith."

And that is the moment I think I feel something of what I imagine Simon felt. For me, it is just a gnawing, tension, but for Simon, it was more like a slap on the face. He had spent the past, how many months, following Jesus around the country. And then, Jesus was talking about a man he had never even met — a Roman man. And he said that this man had more faith than anyone else he had ever met.

Luke told us that Jesus spoke the words and healed the servant then and there, and then went on to do other things. But I have to admit that I am still standing there in the middle of that street looking at that house. I am standing there with Simon, trying to understand what just happened.

Because, you know, as hard as I try to do what I hear Jesus asking me to do, there are times when I see someone or think of someone, and all I can see or think of is Rome. It might be because of what they believe, or something they have done, or some other thing I have used to define them. But as often as I have heard Jesus tell me to love my neighbor, I just cannot find the way to see that person as that neighbor. In my heart, they are, and always will be, Rome.

To think that Jesus might someday point to that person and tell me he had never seen such faith anywhere else, disturbs me. It unsettles me. It makes me wonder if I am still missing something.

It makes me realize that as I try to live my day tending and feeding God's sheep as God has asked me to do, there is something I still need. I need you. I need you to help tend and feed me. I need you to help me stop seeing Romans, and begin seeing only sheep.

Because sometimes I do believe God is asking us to do too much, on our own. And the only way we can truly become the people God is asking us to be is to do it together. And maybe, tending and feeding all of God's sheep, including each other, we can become the people of faith that God is asking us to become. Maybe if we, together, tend and feed God's sheep.

All of them.

All of us.

Together.

Tend and feed.

Tend and feed. Amen.

www.ingramcontent.com/pod-product-compliance
Lightning Source LLC
LaVergne TN
LVHW091158080426
835509LV00006B/739